THE RETIREMENT RACE

Retirement Planning Concepts for
the Race to and through Retirement

Thomas Michael Rauchegger, MBA

Copyright © 2020 by Thomas Michael Rauchegger.

All rights reserved. No part of this publication may be reproduced, distributed or transmitted in any form or by any means, including photocopying, recording or other electronic or mechanical methods, without the prior written permission of the publisher, except in the case of brief quotations embodied in critical reviews and certain other noncommercial uses permitted by copyright law. For permission requests, write to the publisher at the address below.

Thomas Rauchegger/Cramer & Rauchegger, Inc.
800 N Maitland Avenue,
Suite 204
Maitland, FL 32751
https://www.cramerandrauchegger.com/

The Retirement Race/Thomas Michael Rauchegger.—1st edition
ISBN 9798566436401

The contents of this book are provided for informational purposes only and are not intended to serve as the basis for any financial decisions. Any investment, tax, legal or estate planning information is general in nature. It should not be construed as investment, legal or tax advice. Always consult a financial advisor, attorney or tax professional regarding the applicability of this information to your unique situation.

Information presented is believed to be factual and up to date, but we do not guarantee its accuracy, and it should not be regarded as a complete analysis of the subjects discussed. All expressions of opinion are those of the author as of the date of publication and are subject to change. Content should not be construed as personalized financial advice nor should it be interpreted as an offer to buy or sell any financial products mentioned. A qualified financial professional should be consulted before implementing any of the strategies presented. No one strategy can ensure a profit or guarantee against losses in a declining market.

Investing involves risk, including the potential loss of principal. Any references to protection benefits or guaranteed/lifetime income streams refer only to fixed insurance products, not securities or investment products. Insurance and annuity product guarantees are backed by the financial strength and claims-paying ability of the issuing insurance company.

DEDICATION

I dedicate this book to my parents, John and Emma Rauchegger, who came to this country from Austria and Germany, respectively, each with nothing but a bag, strong work ethic, and a whole lot of dreams. They met in New York City, learning English in night school while working during the day as a blue-collar worker and maid. Mom and Dad spent frugally and saved fiercely while investing in themselves. They learned various trades and worked multiple jobs along the way. Eventually, they built a successful chain of beauty salons in New York and Florida (Salon Vienna). Their unconditional love, extraordinary work ethics, and lifelong sacrifices gave me opportunities that I can never fully repay. My parents set many great examples for me so I could become the man, husband, and father I am today. Thank you, Oma and Opa!

I also dedicate this book to my dear wife, Debbie, who has blessed me with her love and support. Debbie has helped me become a better man, husband, and father since we married in 2004. Debbie reintroduced me to my Lord and Savior and helped guide me to become a Christian. This gift is also something I can never repay. Debbie gave birth to our two lovely children, Cassandra and Vaughn. Debbie's success both professionally and in our household has enabled me to focus on my profession, the writing of this book, and helping people reach and maintain their retirement goals every day. Thank you, Debbie!

- Thomas Michael Rauchegger

TABLE OF CONTENTS

FOREWORD i
CHAPTER 1: RACE DAY 1
CHAPTER 2: RETIREMENT PLANNING 7
    It's All About the Income 10
CHAPTER 3: BUILDING A STRONG FINANCIAL HOUSE .. 15
    The Three Pigs and the Big Bad Wolf 17
    Financial House Construction 19
    The Foundation 20
    The Walls 21
    The Roof 22
    The Property 23
CHAPTER 4: RISK-ADJUSTED INVESTING 25
    Lower-Risk Investments 28
    Investments with Risk 28
CHAPTER 5: INCOME PLANNING IN RETIREMENT 35
    Non-Discretionary Spending 37
    Discretionary Spending 38
    Bucket Planning in Retirement 46
CHAPTER 6: TAX PLANNING 49
    Federal Deficit and Debt 49
    Taxability of Investment Accounts 52
CHAPTER 7: ESTATE PLANNING 61
    Probate 63

    Using Beneficiary Designations 63
    Using Special Deeds for Real Estate 64
    Adding Your Children to Your Accounts 64
    Establishing a Revocable Trust 65
    Final Instructions Checklist 67
CHAPTER 8: LIFE INSURANCE 69
CHAPTER 9: LONG-TERM CARE INSURANCE 73
    Self-Insure 75
    Rely on the Government 76
    Traditional Long-Term Care Insurance 77
    Asset-Based Long-Term Care Insurance 78
CHAPTER 10: QUESTIONS YOU SHOULD ASK 81
CHAPTER 11: THE FINISH LINE 89
PICTURES 93
ABOUT THE AUTHOR 97
ACKNOWLEDGMENTS 99

FOREWORD

BY SCOTT CRAMER

Tom and I have been friends for over twenty years. He is the most responsible person that I know. The level of pride that Tom takes in the work he does with our firm, our team, and our clients is only rivaled by the amount of love he has for his wife, children, and parents. I can always count on him to do the right thing. Working with Tom over the last twenty-plus years has been both a personal and a professional privilege.

Most people who come to see us come in because they are concerned about what retirement may look like for them. It may be that their planned retirement is just around the corner, they may have years or decades before they get there, or they may be facing the unexpected end of their career due to factors beyond their control. Regardless, they have one thing in common: They are in our office because they want a real plan.

Of course, in a general way, they know about Social Security. They may have pensions. They know they should plan for unforeseen expenses, and they might even have concerns about investment risks and inflation, but they don't know how to tie all these pieces together in a coherent strategy that will last through their lifetimes.

Many times, on our initial visit with someone, they don't understand how the volatility of their stock market investments can potentially affect their income or whether their money lasts their lifetime. They may have unrealistic assumptions about what an investment can deliver, or an unrealistic picture of the risks they are taking and how they are actually invested.

Clearly, if you have a plan or roadmap, it makes it much easier to navigate your way toward retirement. You can use that plan or roadmap as a metric to measure your progress on a monthly, quarterly, and, of course, annual basis. Sure, you can just try and amass some huge amount of money; that might work, but it is not a plan. And often that is not the most efficient way to prepare for retirement, especially when it comes to withdrawal strategies and taxation. These are the things Tom Rauchegger and I work to address with our clients every day.

Tom has many life experiences that have shaped who he is and how he approaches financial planning. His experience of working in Germany with global markets and his MBA degree helped form the organizational skills he uses with our firm and our clients' retirement goals and plans. As one of the founders of our firm, Tom has really taken ownership and put systems and processes in place to help our firm be more efficient and help deliver quality service and value to our clients.

These processes—a boring word for a vital piece of organization—have differentiated us from other firms. Most other firms scrape together someone's money into a big theoretical pile and use some sort of investment assumption and withdrawal rate to decide a person's retirement income. That is not a plan. Not to put too fine a point on it, but when the market doesn't cooperate with your plans, such as during a recession or global pandemic, those assumptions may be the undoing of your retirement.

Tom and I have built our advisory practice on a different approach: that of understanding our clients' retirement goals on a much more granular basis. We understand their everyday expenses, their one-off maintenance expenses, their dream vacations, and how they want to provide for children and grandchildren. We factor all of this in when we are putting together a plan. Once we understand all of a person's goals, we can build a plan from the ground up and find out exactly what it is that we need to do to each and every year to reach those goals. That means we can structure their assets to get the income they need today while planning for the future. Additionally, we can plan assets to use for future inflation and expenses.

These details matter; they are the stuff of life. As Tom will reiterate throughout this book, retirement isn't about winning some kind of race. It's about your race. As an example, one of our clients told us his retirement dream was for he and his wife to take his whole family—children, grandchildren—on an epic family vacation. For years, he funded a special set of assets to take them on a cruise to Alaska. They rented three adjoining suites, and everyone stayed there together. He described their cruise to me, with the activities they did each day, and how one of the days in particular stood out as a perfect memory, with all family members participating and having fun. That day cost him more than $10,000. He told us this was one of the best days of his and his wife's lives! This shining memory was etched into he and his wife's brains; as he described their time together, he had tears in his eyes. Likely, this memory would also stick with his children and grandchildren for the rest of their lives, as well.

Helping people plan for these kinds of "perfect days" is what we do. They won't look the same for everyone, and financial plans shouldn't all look the same, either.

Tom has put the better part of two years of work and over thirty years of work experience and knowledge into this book, and I can tell you it's a labor of love. While I've told you a bit about what we do in our practice every day, this book is Tom's way of giving the same information and processes we use to inform our work to everyone. Sharing this information is his way of transforming an industry that can often just see people as numbers on paper. We are proud of the practice we have built, and our approach of putting clients' individual selves at the center of what we do.

I am sure the passion for delivering a great retirement and the systematic and practical approach Tom has outlined in this book will help you cross the finish line with the type of retirement you have imagined in your own retirement race.

CHAPTER 1

RACE DAY

It was a beautiful November morning in Central Florida. The air was crisp and the sky bright blue. As the sun rose in the distance, my wife Debbie and I, along with our two children Cassandra and Vaughn, left the house at 7:30 a.m. for a ten-minute drive to Heathrow Elementary school. Although it was a Saturday morning, it felt like another ordinary school day.

We are blessed with two wonderful and healthy children. Cassie, at the time, was eight years old, in third grade, and still dreaming of following in the footsteps of her musical idol, Taylor Swift. Vaughn was a six-year-old, a high energy first grader, whom I am now personally training for the 2030 Men's Soccer World Cup. Vaughn started running when he was nine months old . . . really. He is very athletic. Although he's a little small for his age, he seems to pick up most sports very quickly. He has what I call the three Hs. Vaughn **hates** to lose, he out-**hustles** his opponents, and he plays with his whole **heart.**

As we turned onto Markham Woods Road, cars already lined the streets that lead up to the entrance of the school properties. With the Florida sun rising in the distance, the perfectly clear sky made all the fall colors pop. It was the first county-wide cross country race for Seminole County and we did not want to be late. The kids had brought home a race flyer earlier in the week detailing the race times, special events, and awards for the winners. Debbie and I thought this event would be a great way to start off our weekend and get some early morning exercise behind us. We even promised the kids that, after the race, we would get them the breakfast of champions: a smoothie or a doughnut.

The cross country race was broken into separate groups of boys and girls based on respective age groups, ranging from six to eleven. Each school in the county was represented by their own mix of student runners. Entering the school gates, we noticed the various school flags set up around the field adorned with the different school mascots and colors. The flags made a great place for the runners and parents to meet the coaches before the race.

The kids quickly located their school flag and ran to greet their "runners club" coach and classmates. The coach was registering each student runner into their respective age group while handing out the race bibs. When it was Vaughn's turn to sign in with the coach, I overheard the coach tell Vaughn that she knows he has a lot of energy, and if he races hard, he might even be able to place in the top fifteen and get a medal, or even a trophy. The coach was quite familiar with Vaughn's energy level from P.E. class at school. Maybe she was optimistic about his chances. Personally, I think she was just really good at encouraging the kids.

Then Vaughn asked his coach in front of the other parents and runners, "Where are the trophies?" Without hesitation, the coach turned back toward the school building and pointed to a wall in the distance where a makeshift podium had been set up for the post-race trophy presentations. Vaughn pointed to the podium and responded to the coach, "Meet me over there after the race?" We all laughed out loud at this pre-race exchange.

Like clockwork, it was time for the National Anthem. We all stood at attention as the *Star-Spangled Banner* played over the loudspeakers and echoed in the distance. Emotions overran me; I felt both nervous and excited for all the kids. It was an electrifying atmosphere that reminded me of some of my own childhood races. The crowd gave a loud cheer at the conclusion of the anthem, and it was time for the pre-race music. The theme from the movie *Rocky* got the crowd pumped up as the first group of runners, the six-year-old boys, headed to the starting line to begin their race on the makeshift half-mile cross country track.

Before he left for the starting line, I gave Vaughn his final race instructions and pep talk.

"Run your own race," I said. "No matter what, make sure you finish your race strong!"

The night before, we had talked about the story of the hare and the tortoise, and discussed how running at a consistent speed and then sprinting at the end of the race would get him to the finish line quicker than if he sprinted in the beginning and then had to stop during the race to take a break because he was out of breath. You know how the story goes and how it ends. We were really looking for something *between* a hare and a tortoise. Something like a fast tortoise.

Coach left our group and took the five boys representing our school, including Vaughn, to the starting line. There were about one hundred boys in the entire six-year-old race group. The starting line was packed from one end to the other, and the boys jockeyed for position in the front, as there was not enough space at the starting line for all. I tried to locate Vaughn in the group, but it was very difficult, as they stood about five boys deep.

The racetrack was roped off on both sides and the parents lined it from beginning to end. The horn finally sounded, and the boys took off like rabbits out of the starting gate. For most of them, their half-mile journey around the school grounds would be over in less than ten minutes. The first half of the track was mostly a mix of grass, sand, and dirt with small bumps and hills scattered throughout. The boys started the race packed together in a large group. The track narrowed at the first turn and several crashes took out groups of five to ten boys at a time, who fell and quickly got back up in a haze of dust. Vaughn avoided one of the early crashes while jumping over one of the boys who had tripped and fallen directly in his running path. I tried to visually follow him along the course as long as I could as he found his way to the middle of the pack. Spectators were lined about three people deep along most of the first half of the half mile course, so my vision was mostly impaired. The track then took the boys up a hill and behind the adjacent middle school building. I saw

Vaughn in the distance as he passed several boys going up a small hill, then disappeared behind the school building. Now out of sight, the boys raced onto the asphalt parking lot and eventually around the bus loop.

I positioned myself along the final stretch of the racecourse so I could cheer the boys on as they closed in on the finish line. The final stretch was slightly downhill and a straightaway of about 150 yards through mostly hard sand. As the boys came around the corner of the building and into view, there was Vaughn, now in seventh place and sprinting for the finish line. He passed several bigger boys along the way. He told me later that he passed many boys on that bus loop. He said they started fast and then got tired, just like the hare in the bedtime story.

Vaughn passed two more boys as he sprinted to the finish line. He finished in fifth place with a time of three minutes and twenty-five seconds. As it turns out, only the top five finishers received trophies. I am not sure Vaughn knew that, but he did make good on his promise to his coach. He was the only student representing his school in his age group that placed. Not too bad for his first cross country race! I am sure his recently completed soccer season had not hurt his endurance and energy.

We learned a lot of lessons on our first race day: First, you should run your own individual race and not worry so much about everyone else. We also learned you should practice running leading up to race day and be prepared if you want to have a successful race. Vaughn saw the importance of keeping a consistent pace during the race, and that short sprints and multiple stops would not get him to the finish line faster. In fact, it could delay the finish time. And finally, we learned to always remember to finish strong. It is critical that you don't jeopardize the success of your entire race as you approach the finish line.

Imagine retirement is just like a long race. For some, the "finish line" might be at age fifty-five, while for others it might be at age sixty-five. And for some people, the retirement race may never end. Perhaps they do not feel as if they are in a race, but on a leisurely jog forever and ever. Since getting to retirement for most people means finishing the race somewhere in their mid-to late sixties, I think we can all agree that getting to retirement is like running a very long marathon.

The start of your personal retirement race might begin in your twenties after you have finished high school, trade school, or college and started working full time at your first job or career. Remember, before you decide to enter a race you need to put together a training regimen and a plan to prepare for the race. The same strategies and plan should hold true for your retirement race. If you put together a plan or a "roadmap to retirement" before you start saving and investing, the likelihood of you finishing the race successfully and "on-schedule" will increase exponentially. Remember that everyone's situation and timeline will be different, so you want to be sure you plan to run your own race. Don't be looking over your shoulder and trying to imitate what the other racers are doing. Instead, focus on your own speed and skills. They are unique to you, and you should take advantage of them.

Some people will get married and have children. This will most definitely impact the timeline of their retirement race. These racers will have more short-term costs and expenses than those without children. According to a 2017 report from the U.S. Department of Agriculture, the average cost of raising a child from birth through age seventeen is $233,610. Parents spend between 9 and 22 percent of their total income on childcare.[1]

If you consider the rising costs of post-high-school education, I personally believe the cost of raising a child can quickly increase to a total of well over $300,000.00. This is not necessarily the case for everyone, but as I've observed others' experiences, it can happen. Clearly these expenses will impact parents' retirement savings plan much more than those who do not have children.

Some people start their careers later in life or go back to school. They get additional education or training and then start a second career. This could set your retirement savings plan

---

[1] Smith, Liz. SmartAsset. December 10, 2019. "The Average Cost of Raising a Child." https://smartasset.com/retirement/the-average-cost-of-raising-a-child

back temporarily, but could then spring it forward with an increase in earnings and the ability to save more later.

Some people get out of the starting gate early and others pick up the pace later in the race. But remember to try not to get distracted by everyone else; everyone runs their own retirement race. No matter where you are in age, it is important to put together a budget that will help you understand and prioritize where, and on what, you are spending your money. The best way to start saving is to spend less than you earn over a long period of time and invest the difference. Sounds simple, right?

I remember a conversation with a younger client of the Firm during an annual portfolio review. He had diligently started saving for retirement a few years prior and could see his savings start to build. He had made regular contributions to his retirement accounts over the years, but also saved a large sum of money on the side to add to his portfolio. Once he made the additional investments from those savings, he proudly stated, "I feel like I am now in the race."

This book is designed to help you plan, run, and finish your personal retirement race. It will provide you with some retirement investment strategies and concepts, no matter where you are in your retirement race. These strategies and concepts can also be helpful to you if you have already reached retirement and technically have *finished* your retirement race. I think it is fair to say most people who cross the retirement finish line don't want to get back into the retirement race. As a financial advisor specializing in helping people who are close to or currently enjoying retirement, I have seen a lot, learned a lot, and worked on hundreds of retirement plans over the years for many great individuals and families, and I'd like to share some of my experience and knowledge with you. So please join me now for the next several chapters on our individual journey and race to retirement.

Achtung, fertig, los . . . ready, set, go!

CHAPTER 2

RETIREMENT PLANNING

Have you ever asked, "What is retirement?" Most people probably imagine retirement as one of the happiest times of their lives. After working for decades on end, you finally get the chance to sleep in, travel the world, spend more time with the grandkids, give back to the community, or spend time on the passions you never had the time for while you were working.

One day, my daughter Cassie asked me out of the blue if we would have any money left if we owned three houses. I wondered why she asked me this, but it may have been because we just visited some friends in the North Carolina mountains who own three houses (two of which they use as rental properties).

Kids say and ask the strangest things, don't they? My response was that we probably could own three houses and rent a couple for income, but we only have one house and are trying to save our money so we can enjoy a retirement just like their Oma and Opa (grandparents).

Vaughn responded, "Oma and Opa? They are just lazy. They do whatever they want, play golf, travel to the mountains, and have a whole bunch of money!" I said, "Exactly, that sounds like a pretty good retirement to me." Although I think he may have mistaken having the freedom to not go to work every day unless you choose to do so for being lazy. The truth is my parents worked part-time in retirement for many years and well into their late seventies because that is what they loved to do, and I couldn't get them to stop. My dad and mom are far from "lazy"; they taught me to always work hard and live within my means. They came to this country when they were twenty-one and nineteen years old, respectively. My dad came to the United States from the small country of Austria and my mom came to the United States from a small town in northern Germany. They each landed in New York City, where they eventually met. Both of my parents arrived with nothing but a bag of their possessions, a whole bunch of dreams, and a strong work ethic. My parents made sacrifices for our family, working six days a week, always living within their means, and saving, saving, saving. They are living proof of the American Dream, and I am forever thankful for them!

So: what is retirement planning? Retirement used to look somewhat like this: We were born, went to school, worked our entire lifetimes, and then died quickly after. Retirement was never really a long-term destination, option, or concern for us. Today, people are living much longer lives. Now we are born, go to school, work at our careers, spend years in retirement, and then eventually die; nobody gets out of this life alive. Retirement also used to be a few years in length, and now we need to properly plan for thirty to thirty-five years of retirement living (sometimes a third of our lifetime) as we continue to prosper and live longer lives.

While you are working, generating income is usually an afterthought as long as you are meeting your monthly living expenses and obligations. And when you decide to retire, you should consider retirement as becoming permanently unemployed for the rest of your life. That could mean no salary, wage, or income for thirty to thirty-five years. Without the proper retirement income plan in place, your retirement funds may not see you confidently through your lifetime. Income replacement is therefore crucial in retirement.

If you were to lose your job (layoff, downsizing, etc.) while still in your working years and were unemployed for a few years, imagine the significant impact it would have on your savings and your life. Although it may be temporary, it could set you back for several years. Now imagine that same impact of having no salary for thirty to thirty-five years in retirement. Without proper planning, you might have to go back to work, or worse yet, you might completely run out of money.

It is critical that you properly plan for retirement so, once you have finished your "retirement race," you don't have to get back into the race unless it is on your terms. Remember the adage: "If you fail to plan, you plan to fail." Before you decide to retire, be sure you have saved enough money to support your lifestyle throughout retirement and the rest of your life. In retirement, you will need enough reliable income to meet your monthly needs and replace the lost salary/wage income you had while you were working.

Much has been publicized about the retirement crisis facing America. Inadequate savings, poor or little retirement planning, little understanding of the impact of rising health care costs, longevity, inflation, and the misconceptions about future Social Security benefits: all of these things can have an impact on your retirement race. Unfortunately, I believe people are much more focused today on consuming goods and services rather than planning for their retirements and futures.

About 42 percent of baby boomers have no retirement savings. That is almost half of the boomer population.

Among the baby boomers who have saved for retirement, only about 25 percent think they have enough money to take them through retirement. About 46 percent of all boomers (whether they saved for retirement or not) think they need around $45,000 per year to support them in retirement. And since the average Social Security check is around $17,000, funding will definitely have to come from other income buckets.[2]

---

[2] Insured Retirement Institute. April 10, 2018. "Boomer Expectations for Retirement 2018." https://irionline.org/resources/resources-detail-view/boomer-expectations-for-retirement-2018

Those who enter retirement with no savings, no pensions, and no income beyond Social Security will find it difficult to match their expectations to their resources. They'll likely need to delay full retirement and continue working full- or part-time for longer than they had planned. They may be forced to accept a lower standard of living in retirement than they were accustomed to in their working years or which they expected to have in retirement.

Retirees who have done the proper retirement planning and saved for their retirement years appear to be in much better shape by several measures including financial assets, expenses, and health status. Retirees who have little or no debt also seem to fair much better in retirement. Having low or no fixed costs allows you more flexibility with your discretionary spending. If you do not have a mortgage, rent, or car payment (usually the highest monthly expenses), then your fixed monthly income needs in retirement will be significantly lower and much more manageable. In our financial advisory practice, we often say that those with little or no debt have the best retirements. I've seen this to be true over time.

It's All About the Income

Retirement isn't all about sailboats and golf courses. At least, that's not what the one in four Americans who fear outliving their income think. That's according to a survey by the Indexed Annuity Leadership Council, which also found that nearly one in five Americans don't have a clue about how much they've saved for retirement.[3]

It used to be that companies offered defined-benefit plans (think pensions) for their most loyal employees. As an example, my father-in-law worked for an insurance company for thirty-five years, and when he retired, he was awarded a healthy retirement package that included a corporate pension that would

---

[3] Indexed Annuity Leadership Counsel. 2020. "Americans' Top Three Retirement Fears." https://fiainsights.org/retirement-fears/

pay him a monthly income for the rest of his and his wife's lifetimes. It also used to be that people worked for one company for most of their entire career. Today, rarely can you find a private sector company that offers its employees (loyal or not) a pension when they retire. So, for most people, today you are truly on your own when it comes to planning for and saving for your retirement.

Pensions have been replaced with the more common corporate 401(k), or similar defined-contribution retirement plans. Today, pensions are primarily offered to employees of state or federal governments.

This puts a very large burden on today's workers. The responsibility to mandatorily save and grow your money now shifts from the employer to the employee. In addition, most corporate defined-contribution plans (401(k)s, etc.) offer only investment options (usually a basket of mutual funds) in the stock and bond markets. If you only save for your retirement through your company-sponsored retirement plan, you may be in for a bumpy ride that is solely dependent on the performance of the markets over time, and then you will still have to deal with taxation when you withdraw the money.

Consider the difference between building capital and building income. While you are working and saving money in your retirement accounts, your focus is on building capital. Once you retire, your focus must shift toward preserving capital and building income instead. That's an entirely different mindset, and it requires you to play by different rules than the rules you used when building your capital.

What makes things even more complicated is the rules can change depending on the economy, the market, inflation, taxes, and several other factors. For most people, this will mean having to fill a "retirement income gap." A retirement income gap is the difference, or gap, between your fixed income and your expenses in retirement. What is the percentage of total capital you can safely withdraw from your retirement accounts each year to fill this retirement income gap without eventually running out of money?

How about 4 percent of your capital? The 4 percent rule was first introduced in 1994 by financial advisor Bill Bengen, and quickly became conventional wisdom. Since the early 1990s, most experts have adopted the rule of thumb that if you withdraw 4 percent of the balance in your retirement accounts each year, your accounts will last you at least thirty years in retirement.[4]

Unfortunately, because of the ever-changing economic conditions, stock market performance for the past twenty or so years, sustained low interest rates, rising health care costs, overall cost of living increases, etc., the 4 percent rule may no longer be as reliable as it once was.

If you retire at age sixty or sixty-five, it's entirely possible that you will live longer than thirty years in retirement. There's also evidence that, in a sustained low interest rate environment, a 4 percent withdrawal rate is too high and will cause your funds to run out well before the thirty-year mark in retirement. Many large financial institutions and retirement experts have reduced their estimated withdrawal percentages from 4 percent down to 3.5 percent. Keep in mind this withdrawal rate does not consider any legacy plan you may have in mind to leave some of your wealth to the next generations (likely your children and grandchildren).

So, how do you plan for a worry-free retirement with the absence of a corporate or government pension, or even with a pension that does not include a cost-of-living adjustment to keep up with inflation? What about Social Security? Can you solely rely on Social Security for your retirement income? Many retirees believe so. The reality is that Social Security was never designed to provide a long-term income benefit for retirement. Because of the combination of people living longer, taking Social Security benefits before full retirement age (early at age sixty-two), and an underfunded system, you cannot solely rely on Social Security as your only retirement income source.

Even the the Social Security Administration thinks so. According to an excerpt posted on the Social Security website

---

[4] Bloomberg. February 4, 2019. "An Update on the 4% Rule." https://www.investmentnews.com/an-update-on-the-4-rule-78016

(www.ssa.gov), Social Security benefits are not intended to be your only source of income when you retire. For an average, middle-class household, Social Security will replace about 40 percent of your annual pre-retirement earnings. You will need other additional savings, investments, pensions, or retirement accounts to make sure you have enough money to live comfortably when you retire.[5] What will Social Security look like when you retire? What income benefits can you rely on when you retire?

Go to www.ssa.gov and check on your estimated future Social Security benefits so you can properly plan for retirement. When to start taking Social Security benefits is also a very important decision and will effect the amount of benefits you receive (and potentially how much your spouse will receive) for your lifetimes. This decision can have a large impact, either positive or negative, on your overall retirement income plan.

---

[5] Social Security Administration. 2020. "Understanding the Benefits." https://www.ssa.gov/pubs/EN-05-10024.pdf

CHAPTER 3

BUILDING A STRONG FINANCIAL HOUSE

As you plan and save for retirement, or if you are currently in retirement, you should consider looking at your complete financial portfolio in a way that is similar to the construction of a house. Let's call it our financial house. If you are going to build a house, you'll want to build a house that can weather all the elements and stand strong in both the good times and the bad times. Houses are usually constructed to last a long, long time.

Homeowners all over the world live in areas that are susceptible to different kinds of inclement weather, including hurricanes, tornados, earthquakes, fires, flooding, winter snow and ice storms, and more. They face the challenge of constructing a home that can weather all of these elements. Even in the Sunshine State of Florida, we have had our share of devastating hurricanes, tornados, and even power outages in recent years.

You should look at building your investment portfolio in the same manner. Over time, your financial assets must be able to weather a multitude of uncertain conditions and events, including stock market volatility, economic downturns, fluctuating interest rates, rising inflation, global economics, political turmoil, and even personal changes in your own life.

Building a strong, flexible, renewable, and sustainable retirement investment portfolio is a lot like building a weather-resistant home. The overall strength of a house is dependent on how well its components (walls, roof, and foundation) work together as a single structure and unit.

THE STRONG FINANCIAL HOUSE

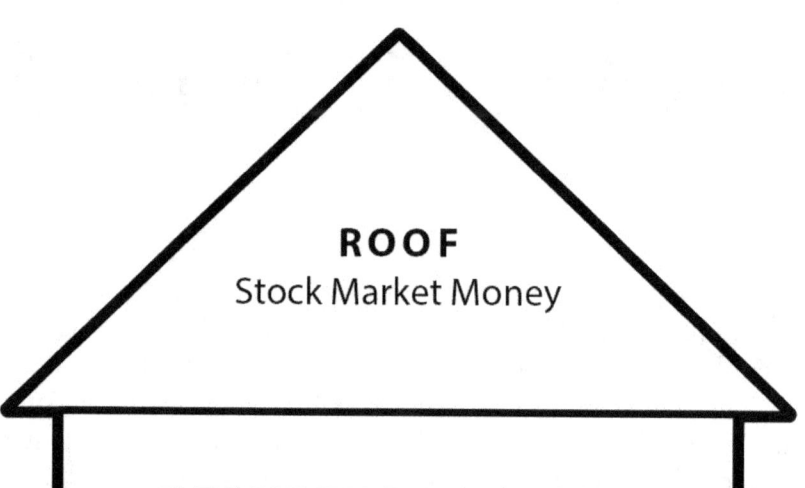

What does your financial house look like? How much money do you have in the roof? How much do you have in the walls? Does your house have a strong foundation?

The Three Pigs and the Big Bad Wolf

Do you remember the story of the three pigs and the big bad wolf? There are several lessons to be learned from this fairy tale. My children, Cassie and Vaughn, still love to hear stories at bedtime. My wife, Debbie, and I took turns at night telling them stories about our childhoods or reading them fairytale books. As toddlers, their favorite bedtime story was the Three Pigs and the Wolf. This story has several lessons we can learn from, even when it comes to retirement planning and building your strong financial house.

When I would cuddle up in bed at night with my daughter, Cassie, and tell her the story, it usually went something like this:

There were three brother pigs who grew up and ventured into the world, leaving mom and dad behind as they set out for fame and fortune. The youngest pig stopped at the side of the road and decided to build himself a house made of straw. He did not put much effort into the construction of his house, nor did it cost him substantial time or energy. His house stood strong during the good times, but one day he received a knock on the door from a visitor. It was a hungry wolf. He told the pig to come out, but the pig was frightened. The wolf threatened to huff and puff and blow the house down if the pig would not come out. The pig was too scared to leave the house and did not want to be the wolf's next meal. So, the wolf huffed and puffed and blew the straw house down. Devastated, the pig ran off into the forest searching for his two older brothers.

The youngest pig eventually came across his middle brother's house. The middle pig spent a little more time, energy, and effort when he built his house in the forest. He gathered wood and built his house stronger than the straw house his younger brother had constructed. The two brothers lived together, and life was good until one day they received a knock on the door. Again, it was the hungry wolf who told the pigs to come out, or he would huff and puff and blow their house down. Naturally, they stayed inside, and the wolf eventually huffed and puffed and blew down the shaky wooden house. Frightened, the two pigs ran for their lives into the dark forest.

The brothers came across the house of their oldest brother. He was a very smart pig and actually took the time to design his house before he began construction. He designed and planned his house so it could withstand both the good and bad times. He built the house on a strong foundation with bricks and mortar, put up wooden stabilized walls and then finished off his house with a secure roof. Now the brothers were back together again, enjoying life as a family living in comfort in the securely built house. One night, the pigs were enjoying a meal, singing and dancing together when *they were interrupted by a knock at the door. It was that wolf again, and he was hungrier than ever. He told the pigs that if they did not come out, he would huff and puff and blow down their house. Frightened, once again the pigs decided to stay in their house and take their chances. This time the wolf huffed and puffed, but the house stood strong. The oldest pig clearly took the time to plan out, design, and build his house in a manner that would weather almost any storm—or a surprise visit from a hungry wolf.*

What can we learn financially from this old fairy tale? Let's start by putting a retirement plan together before you begin the construction of your financial house. Working with a financial advisor to blueprint your plan is a great start. It is often said that if you want to reach a goal, you need to have a plan. The most important takeaway is, if you construct a strong financial house, your retirement has a better chance of sustaining you during both good and uncertain economic times.

Financial House Construction

When you begin building a house, you start with a full set of construction drawings to plan out the details of your home. This is the blueprint that shows not only what your house will look like, but all the individual components that will integrate to create the home. Obviously, you don't start with one room and then add on from there. You design the whole house at one time. To do so, you must first consider all of your objectives for the house. Do you want a highly energy-efficient home? Perhaps you will need to plan for solar panels. Or, if you're concerned about having your home be safe, you may plan for a safe room. You will also consider what you *don't* want in your house, such as high-maintenance carpet flooring.

With these objectives in mind, you and a professional designer would work together to draw up a plan that includes every room and every component of each room—electrical, plumbing, cabinetry, etc.—until you have a full set of construction plans, including a list of materials and resources needed to build your house.

Similarly, a solid retirement portfolio should comprise a foundation, walls, and a roof. This is exactly how the smart elder pig protected himself and his house from the hungry wolf. The first component of your financial house should be the foundation. Without a strong foundation, your financial house may crumble in uncertain economic times. The Bible references this in Matthew 7:24-26, in a parable of wise and foolish builders.

> "Everyone then who hears these words of mine and does them will be like a wise man who built his house on the rock. And the rain fell, and the floods came, and the winds blew and beat on that house, but it did not fall, because it had been founded on the rock. And everyone who hears these words of mine and does not do them will be like a foolish man who built his house on the sand."

The Foundation

Let us learn from the parable of the wise and foolish builders and build our financial house on a strong foundation. The foundational elements of a retirement portfolio are typically the most protected assets, which is the money you cannot afford to lose. This is the money that is used to pay living expenses and act as an emergency fund now and in the future. In the retirement portfolio, the walls and especially the roof could be rebuilt over time if losses were suffered, but the foundation needs to provide stability for the rest of the house.

Your Foundation should generally be composed of accounts and investments that are protected from losses (principal protected). These can include, but are not limited to, the following:
- Checking, savings and money market accounts at an FDIC insured bank or credit union
- Certificates of Deposit (CDs) issued by an FDIC insured bank or credit union

- Government bonds backed by the U.S. Treasury Department
- Traditional fixed annuities backed by the financial strength and claims-paying ability of the issuing insurance company
- Fixed index annuities, backed by the financial strength and claims-paying ability of the issuing insurance company

These are just a few examples of foundational investments, but I think you get the idea. Warren Buffett is often quoted as saying there are two rules to investing. Rule No. 1: Never lose money, and Rule No. 2: Never forget Rule No. 1.[6] The foundation of your financial house helps you adhere to this rule and can at the same time help you maintain a reliable income stream in retirement, which we will address later in our retirement race.

The Walls

The walls of a retirement portfolio represent the first level of risk in a portfolio. The walls can be composed of investments that can provide various benefits including diversification, income, and growth, but are not as conservative as the financial vehicles in the foundation.

Investments in the walls can be non-stock-market-correlated as they coordinate with investments in the foundation and the roof. These investments can also contribute significantly to your goals with different, and sometimes moderate, risk through additional diversification, offering the potential for both growth and income options as well as flexibility. Some of the securities that could compose part of the walls of a retirement portfolio include the following:

- Corporate bonds
- Municipal bonds
- Senior notes and loans

---

[6] Stephanie Loiacono. Investopedia. June 30, 2019. "Rules That Warren Buffet Lives By." https://www.investopedia.com/financial-edge/0210/rules-that-warren-buffett-lives-by.aspx

- Private debt (business development companies)
- Personal loans
- Private equity
- Private real estate (real estate investment trusts)
- Personal rental property
- Oil and gas (energy)
- Commodities

The Roof

The roof of your financial house is often represented by the highest level of risk in your portfolio. Some people have larger roofs than others based on their risk preference and personal situation (age and timeline to retirement). The securities in the roof have opportunity to grow, but the principal can also go down in value (suffer losses) because of external forces beyond our control, like the way wind, rain, or hail might damage the roof to your house during a severe storm.

This is the reason you should start the construction of your retirement portfolio with a sound foundation and strong walls. Should your roof be damaged and suffer losses due to the risk-based investments, it should not cause your house to crumble. The roof can be replaced or repaired over time as is the case with your personal home. Some of the securities that may be a part of your roof could include the following:

- Stocks
- Exchange-traded funds (ETFs)
- Mutual funds
- Interval funds
- Options
- Managed accounts
- Investment options in your 401(k), retirement plans, etc.

The Property

Finally, to help protect your future and that of your loved ones against potential portfolio losses that may occur before or after your death, you may want to consider building a fence around your house. Life insurance and long-term care insurance are some of the fence-like instruments you may want to consider as offering a type of fiscal house preservation and protection.

Life insurance can be used to replace income for an unexpected or premature death. It can also be used to transfer wealth to the next generation with tax advantages, or even potentially provide tax-free retirement income.

It should be noted that tax-free income from life insurance is the result of policy loans and withdrawals, which will reduce the policy's death benefit and cash values, and could cause the policy to lapse or require additional premiums to remain in force, depending on the amount of loans or withdrawals. For this reason, you will want to manage your policy's performance and cash values carefully to ensure it remains in force.

Long-term care insurance can help protect a financial house against the potential future costs of a long-term care catastrophe or need. We will review these two concepts, life insurance and long-term care insurance, in much greater detail later in our race to retirement.

If you have children, you may also want to build a pool or playground on your property, which for your fiscal house might translate to college savings plans and educational planning for the future, and the investments that can help us achieve these goals.

CHAPTER 4

RISK-ADJUSTED INVESTING

In my wealth management practice, we believe there are four key areas that make up total wealth management for the prudent retiree. These include risk-adjusted investing, income planning, tax planning, and estate planning. These four areas should all be addressed while putting together a retirement plan and all four areas should work together as part of a coherent strategy.

Remember Warren Buffett's rules of investing I referenced earlier in the book? Rule No. 1: Never lose money, and Rule No. 2: Never forget Rule No. 1. The reality is that each investor is different from the other and each person has their own comfort and tolerance level for the amount of investment risk they are willing to take.

I have lived most of my life in Central Florida, within close proximity to the Disney parks. Several years ago, my wife Debbie and I decided to do a staycation and take the kids to Disney's Magic Kingdom. Now, it should be noted that Cassie and Vaughn have little fear when it comes to amusement park rides. I remember waiting patiently in line for the Big Thunder Mountain Railroad rollercoaster and then getting to the checkpoint, hoping Vaughn would make the height cutoff. Vaughn, standing as straight and tall as he could muster, just barely made the minimum height cutoff so we could all ride together.

After we rode the big drops, bumpy tracks, and hairpin turns, I realized how much more I enjoyed roller coasters when I was a young kid as opposed to a middle-aged father. I started thinking about how similar retirement and investing can be when comparing the different rides at Disney World. Some retirees seek the thrills and spills of the big hills while others choose a steady, smoother, and more predictable ride like the Monorail. I fear that with age I have become more of a Monorail guy than a Thunder Mountain rider.

If you look at the S&P 500 stock market index between January 1, 2000 and March 31, 2020, the index returned a total of 76 percent over those twenty years, and all the gains came over the last seven years.[7] That is an annualized return of less than 3.8 percent. It might not sound like enough when you remember having to endure the big drops of the S&P 500 from September 2000 through October 2002 (an approximate loss of 48 percent) and from October 2008 through March 2009 (an approximate loss of 57 percent)—and, of course, at the time this book was being written, it dropped 20 percent in Q1 of 2020 and 32 percent between February 19, 2020 and March 22, 2020 (during the COVID-19 pandemic).

If you had the option of riding either the Monorail or Thunder Mountain throughout retirement, which one would you choose? I guess the answer to that question might depend on where you are in your retirement race. Are you just starting out or getting close to the finish line? We are told the stock market always goes up over a long period of time, and that may be true, but what is a long period of time? Ten, twenty, fifty, or even one hundred years? And, more importantly, how does this timeline, risk, and its potential volatility fit into your overall retirement savings and income plan?

Many people plan to retire in their mid- to late sixties. That means, when you retire, you just might be permanently unemployed for thirty-plus years. Many retirees draw both principal

---

[7] Yahoo! Finance. 2020. "S&P 500 Historical Data." https://finance.yahoo.com/quote/%5EGSPC/history/

and interest from retirement savings in order to pay their living expenses and maintain the lifestyle to which they have become accustomed. If the market is dropping and you are still drawing from your stock market investments, you may begin drawing down too much of your interest and principal to maintain the same lifestyle. This could potentially jeopardize your lifestyle and maybe even your entire retirement plan.

The retiree seeking a smoother and more predictable ride should consider establishing a growth and income plan built upon a combination of stock market, fixed-return, and non-stock-market-correlated investments. Allocating your life savings in short, medium, and long-term investments can also help mitigate the need to take money out of an investment at the absolute worst time and help you avoid those big drops in your portfolio during uncertain times.

Most people have worked hard and saved diligently for more than forty years so they can travel, spend time with the grandkids, enjoy their life passions, and maintain their lifestyles without worrying about the next turn or drop. If you are currently in retirement, you may want to stay on track to meet those goals so you can continue to enjoy your retirement. The wilder or higher-risk ride might be fitting when you are young and still working, but the less risky and more confident ride may better suit the retiree.

I played soccer most of my life including six years in Germany in the Bavarian League. I learned the importance of defense. Experts say defense wins a lot of championships, and I would add that defense also wins a lot of games. In Germany, where soccer is king, I learned firsthand how important it is to play the game of soccer with your mind on defense. I remember our coach preaching this to our players in the locker room before several of our games. "If they don't score, we do not lose." It sounds funny, but he was right. If you do not let the other team score, it is tough to lose games. That is not only true in soccer. If you can avoid big losses with your retirement investments, your retirement can be more assured. The way to accomplish this is to manage your investment risk.

Risk is a measure of how much you can lose or are willing to lose. In plain speech, how much of a loss can you stomach and how will those losses impact you? There are several different ways to measure investment risk; however, the most basic method is to ask yourself if you can lose with this investment, and to what degree.

Lower-Risk Investments

A conservative investor may seek the guarantees of a bank issued CD (certificate of deposit) offering FDIC (Federal Deposit Insurance Corporation) insurance. Depending on the interest rate environment, the bank may offer you very low interest rates. Fixed rate annuities, issued and backed by the financial strength and claims-paying ability of insurance companies, offer single or multi-year fixed interest rates. Money in checking, savings, and money market accounts is also not subject to losses, but, depending on prevailing interest rates, sometimes these products do not offer attractive rates of return.

Investments with Risk

Every investment other than the aforementioned bank and insurance company products has some varying degree of risk. For example, investing in a single stock (which represents equity in a company) may offer you a high possible rate of return on your investment. Imagine if you had invested a lot of money in Apple Stock back in the nineties, and held on to it. You would probably be rich today. In the late nineties, many of us were investing in technology stocks, seeking the home run stocks while trying to avoid the strikeout stocks.

When I was getting my Executive M.B.A. at the University of Central Florida back in 1998, one of my colleagues, who worked for Nestlé at the time, tapped me on the shoulder during class one day and passed me a small piece of paper and written on it was the name "Amazon." My classmate, Chris, was very excited about Amazon's potential and wanted to share it with me. I can still hear his voice saying, "Tom, the money is in Amazon. Amazon baby, it is a no brainer." Well, I think it is safe to say that Chris was right about Amazon, and yes, I did buy some Amazon stock, and was very happy about it.

The opposite could have happened to you had you invested in the widely held and very popular Enron stock that eventually became worthless in the 2000s. Had you bought Enron, you could have lost your entire investment. Little did I realize at the time, but years after the Enron debacle, we were visited in our practice by a former employee of Enron who had put most all her 401(k) retirement contributions and savings into Enron company stock. She had worked for Enron for several years, starting off as an administrator and then working her way up through the company ranks. She explained to us that at one time her 401(k) was worth over $2 million, most of it in Enron stock. She told us that at the time she was in great financial shape to retire comfortably and had expected to work one or two more years, never imagining the potential risk she was taking. Ultimately, and sadly, she lost it all and was not able to retire. She even shared with us a picture of herself in the local newspaper, testifying before Congress during the Enron trials. These two situations, the Amazon home run and the Enron strikeout, are extreme examples of the potential risks when it comes to investing, but they are true and real.

For many years, the investor's rule of thumb concerning risk and risk-adjusted investing was to take your age and subtract it from 100. That was the percentage of your investment portfolio you could afford to have in risky investments. For example: If you are seventy years of age, based on this rule you should have a maximum of 30 percent invested in risky investments. Based on this rule of thumb, if you are forty years of age you can have up to 60 percent invested in risky investments. The premise is that, the older you get, the less time you will have to make up for potential investment losses, so it is critical to avoid losses as much as you can in your later years of life. This is a general rule of thumb only. Your percentage of money exposed to the market and your overall risk level will vary by your unique situation.

In addition, make sure you do not have what is known as concentration risk, which is what happens when you have too much money of your entire investment savings in any one investment (for example, a single stock or fund). Generally, in our practice, we recommend not having more than 10 percent of your overall investment savings portfolio in any one stock. Sometimes, in very special circumstances, such as discounted stock options you receive while working for a company, this can be increased to 20 percent.

Back in 2000, we had a potential client visit us who had worked for a branch of GE and had amassed over $1.7 million of GE stock in his 401(k). He was about to retire and had over 50 percent of his liquid net worth tied up in the GE stock position. At the time GE stock was worth over $58 per share. After speaking with our Firm, he decided to liquidate the stock position and put together a retirement growth and income plan with investment diversification to help protect himself against concentration risk in one stock.

In 2018, GE stock was worth less than $13 per share. If he had kept the GE stock position, he would have lost $1.3 million and it would have derailed his retirement and changed his life forever. To be fair, it could have gone the other way, too, and GE could have doubled over this same time period, but that would not have changed his life nearly as much as losing that money would have. Remember the saying "Don't have all of your eggs in one basket"? Is it worth the risk to have all your eggs in one basket, no matter how good the stock or investment may or may not be? What happens if the basket drops in value, like GE?

While diversification can't ensure a profit or guarantee that you won't lose money, investing in different types of securities over time, both stock-market- and non-stock-market-correlated, helps lower the overall risk to your investment portfolio, helping to reduce your potential losses in a prolonged downturn in order to increase your long-term investment returns.

It can potentially take many years to accumulate a meaningful gain in an investment. Unfortunately, it's possible that those gains could be wiped out by a single bear market cycle or unpredictable event. A 100 percent gain accumulated over a seven- to ten-year period would be completely eroded by a 50 percent loss. Market corrections can happen at any time, including at the time when you need your money the most—in retirement.

In percentage terms, gains and losses are not equal. You will need a 100 percent gain to get back to even after a 50 percent loss. You will need a 67 percent gain to negate a 40 percent loss. A 30 percent loss will require a 43 percent gain just to get back to even. When it comes to growing and preserving your wealth, half may be worth more to you. Don't be confused by this math.

I mentioned earlier in the book the adage of not having all your eggs in one basket. You can be extremely diverse in your stock selection, but if you are only invested in stocks then it is still just one basket. Remember, the S&P 500 index itself is very diverse—it includes 500 companies representing the large-cap segment of the U.S. equities market. But those companies often rise and fall in a similar pattern.

This reminds me of a lovely couple that visited our firm back in December 2007. To keep them anonymous, I will refer to them as the Smiths. If you remember the conditions of the economy, real estate, and stock market back then, there was a lot of optimism. The stock market went up significantly between 2004 and 2007. Investors forgot about the stinging stock market downturn from 2000 to 2003, where the market lost over 50 percent of its value and the technology space suffered even heavier losses.

Back in 2006, unemployment was decreasing, real estate prices hit their peak (both commercially and residentially), banks were lending liberally to anyone, people were buying and selling (flipping) real estate properties, which drove the costs/values above true market values, the federal government was raising interest rates, inflation was increasing, and there was strong optimism that there was no end to the increasing returns of both the stock and real estate markets in sight.

In December of 2007, the Smiths were referred to us and attended one of our educational dinner events. They visited our office and showed us the portfolio they had amassed over forty-five years of hard work and saving. The Smiths had done everything right. They put their kids through college and trade schools, paid off their mortgage, and saved, saved, saved. And the Smiths did this on middle-class wages. They were careful with their spending, always spent less than they made, and saved the difference. They were one year from the end of their retirement race. Mr. Smith explained his last day of work was going to be December 31, 2008.

Mr. and Mrs. Smith talked about their retirement plans with us. They had sacrificed for so long, and they had a bucket list of places they were going to travel to around the world. They also planned to spend time with the grandkids who were living out of state. They showed us their portfolio and life savings. They had amassed approximately $1 million in retirement savings. During the analysis of their portfolio, we noticed that they had one major problem. They had 95 percent (or approximately $950,000) of their life savings invested in mutual funds between their retirement and non-retirement accounts, with the remaining amount (5 percent, or approximately $50,000) invested in cash or cash-like instruments. Their retirement income plan was to live off the combined Social Security income and the interest of their savings and investments. We told them that they had plenty of money to last their lifetime based on their expenses and the lifestyle they wanted to maintain in retirement . . . as long as they did not lose their money. We also explained they were very close to the finish line of their retirement race (one year to go) and any losses they suffered between now and then could be detrimental to their retirement plans.

We also shared with them that their current mutual fund investments did not match their risk preference or retirement goals. The analysis showed that, on a risk scale of 0 to 100 percent (with 100 percent being the highest), their current portfolio had them at an 88 percent. Their risk matched that of an average young investor with twenty years from the end of their retirement race as opposed to one year. We explained that a market correction or downturn could be a significant hit to their retirement plans and timeline. They were astounded by this information as they stated, "Our current broker never talked about risk in these terms." We scheduled a follow-up appointment for them so we could put a plan in place to help protect their life's savings, to implement some changes to the portfolio that would more closely match their true risk comfort level, and construct a retirement income plan for their retirement years.

For most people, as they get closer to retirement, they should be more concerned about preserving their nest egg rather than getting the best return. For the Smiths, it would be especially important, as they were about to go from an accumulation stage of investing (contribution) to a distribution stage of investing (withdrawal). They needed a growth and income plan to supplement their Social Security income and it was time to start making the adjustments. Mr. and Mrs. Smith were very nervous about their situation and excited about learning more about the details of a retirement income plan.

Unfortunately, the day before our follow-up appointment, the Smiths called us. They shared with us a conversation they had with their stockbroker at the time. He explained to them that they had been working together for many years, the mutual funds that they owned were conservative in nature and well diversified. He said they were right on track to having a great retirement. He told them, "Why would you want to make any adjustments now? The market is on fire and you do not want to miss out on any returns in the coming year!" They thanked us for all the time we spent with them and the thorough analysis we did for them, but gracefully cancelled their follow-up appointment with us, and said that they were staying where they were at and with their current advisor.

We all know what happened starting in the third week of September of 2008, and what continued until the first week of March in 2009. The S&P 500 lost over 50 percent of its value in just a few weeks, the banks tightened up lending, real estate sales froze overnight, and real estate values continued decreasing even more quickly. It was a very scary time in our nation's history. Without government and fiscal bailouts, the financial disaster of 2008 could have been even worse.

For many people it was just a huge loss. Some people lost as much as half of their lifesavings, retirement savings, and wealth in a few months. Many financial advisors, banks, and real estate companies went out of business. People lost their jobs, rental properties, and even their personal homes. It was particularly difficult for retirees and soon-to-be retirees. The Smiths came back to see us in early March of 2009 and not surprisingly they were not retired and had ridden the market all the way down. Their million dollars of savings turned into approximately $550,000. There was really nothing we could do for them but wait for the market to come back. Imagine doing the right thing for forty-five years and then losing half of your life savings in a few months. Truly, the Smiths lost something even more precious than money. They lost *time*, and that is something you can never get back.

This severe market downturn came at the worst possible time for the Smiths, just as they were nearing the end of their long retirement race; the finish line was in sight. To this day, I often wonder about the Smiths, if we could have been more convincing at the time, and how they ultimately fared in their retirement race.

CHAPTER 5

INCOME PLANNING IN RETIREMENT

Your actual net worth becomes less meaningful when you retire. You might have diligently been setting aside money for the future and have a big nest egg now. But even one million dollars might not last long in retirement if you live in a state where the cost of living is high or if you just spend a lot of money. Unfortunately, in my experience, when people set retirement savings goals, they often do so without knowing how much they'll need each month to cover expenses in retirement. Only 38 percent of workers have estimated how much income they would need each month in retirement, according to a survey by the Employee Benefit Research Institute and Greenwald & Associates.[8] What really matters is how much income your net worth will produce for you in retirement.

Don't forget, it is still all about the income in retirement. Do you know how much your retirement will cost you? Have you

---

[8] EBRI and Greenwald & Associates. 2018. "2018 Retirement Confidence Survey." https://www.ebri.org/docs/default-source/rcs/1_2018rcs_report_v5mgachecked.pdf?sfvrsn=e2e9302f_2

considered how you will pay for it? Do you know how to generate the retirement income you will need? For many current and future retirees, these can be daunting questions. Unfortunately, many people put off addressing these questions until it is far too late.

So, exactly how much will retirement cost? Well, we can learn a lot from the numbers. Currently the *median* (or middle) income for all retirees is around $43,500. However, the *average* retirement income is around $67,000.[9] Of course, what you will need will depend on who you are, so you might want to simply calculate your current expenses like housing, transportation, health care, food, insurance, gifting and entertainment.

For starters, don't automatically assume that you'll spend a lot less in retirement. In my experience, many retirees spend about 80 to 90 percent of what they were spending during the year before they retired. In our financial practice, we ask clients during their first visit with us how much they spend on a monthly or annual basis and many, many times we get "the deer in the headlights" look. How can this be? The amount you want to realistically spend in retirement on a monthly basis is arguably the most important number you need to know.

Some people know this figure down to the penny, some have created spreadsheets, while others have an approximate idea and others simply have no clue. Most people have never put a pen to paper or a finger to keyboard and done the math. Remember, when you retire you are permanently unemployed and will need to replace your salary and wages so you can pay your expenses and maintain your lifestyle. How do you know the amount of income you will need if you don't know how much you are spending? Personal Finance 101 starts with calculating your income versus your expenses. No matter where you are in your retirement race, you should create a personal budget (or expense log) so you know exactly how much your total expenses are on a monthly and annual basis.

---

[9] Kathleen Coxwell. NewRetirement. January 21, 2020. "Average Retirement Income 2020: How Do You Compare?" https://www.newretirement.com/retirement/average-retirement-income-2020-how-do-you-compare/

ING had a very popular TV advertisement several years ago that asked the question, "What is your number?" The number referenced in the TV advertisement was how much money you needed to save prior to retirement to have enough money to comfortably last your lifetime. The commercial asked, Is your number $500,000, or $1 million, or perhaps $3 million?

Your number will largely be impacted by two factors in retirement: spending (expenses) and income. I think the ING advertisement should have really asked a different question, "What is your expense, or spending, number?" Let's focus some time on the spending aspect of retirement planning. There are four main areas to consider when calculating your income needs and future spending in retirement:
- Non-discretionary spending
- Discretionary spending
- Inflation
- Life expectancy

Non-Discretionary Spending

Non-discretionary spending is your "must have" spending, which is generally out of your control. These include the day-to-day expenses you spend to maintain your standard of living. These living expenses include everything from groceries to gas to the electric bill.

Debt expenses usually include a mortgage, a home equity line of credit, car loans, student loans, and credit card debt. Anything you owe money on needs to be considered when mapping out your expenses, and some of these expenses will hopefully go away in the future, such as a mortgage payment, school loan, or monthly savings for a child's college.

While taxes are often lower for retirees as they shift from salaried income to capital gains and dividend income tax rates, the government still always seems to get its cut. Many retirees who receive a pension in retirement and/or have their money mostly saved in pre-taxed investment accounts such as IRAs, 401(k)s, 457(b)s, 403(b)s, etc., find they are actually not in a lower tax bracket in retirement, especially once they start making withdrawals from their taxable accounts.

Health care costs are also a major consideration for many in retirement. In fact, along with Social Security, it is one of the top retirement concerns for the baby boomer generation.[10] If you retire prior to age sixty-five you will most likely need to pay for your own health insurance, and these costs have historically risen faster than inflation. Health insurance costs have become a larger share of total expenses for retirees over the last several years. At age sixty-five, retirees do become Medicare eligible and the Medicare supplemental insurance premium costs are usually significantly lower than private health insurance premiums. However, Medicare supplemental insurance policy premiums have also increased over time due to the overall rising costs of health care.

Discretionary Spending

Beyond basic living expenses is what you might think of as your "want to have" spending. This type of spending is also known as discretionary spending. Discretionary spending is subject to each person's personal situation. Great examples of discretionary spending may include satellite TV, a golf membership at a country club, or travel expenses. If a discretionary spending item becomes a "can't live without," then it becomes part of the non-discretionary spending.

Many people have a bucket list of travel destinations when they retire. Trips may include visiting kids and grandkids out of state or abroad, annual cruises, or a summer trip to Europe. We have a client that took his entire family—including kids and grandkids—on an Alaskan cruise one summer. In his words, they "had the time of their lives and made memories that will last several lifetimes."

---

[10] Maurie Backman. The Motley Fool via *USA TODAY*. April 26, 2018. "Retirement concerns: Health care costs, Social Security have Baby Boomers worried most." https://www.usatoday.com/story/money/personalfinance/retirement/2018/04/26/2-retirement-concerns-baby-boomers-worried-most/34158541/

Retirement can also be a great time to start a hobby or rekindle an old one. Like any other activity, hobbies can incur some costs and need to be planned for in retirement as part of your monthly and annual expenses.

Are you not retired, or even close to retirement yet? Calculating a yearly budget and knowing where you are spending your money is a great idea, no matter where you are in your personal retirement race. Doing this will also give you the information you need so you can properly "save the difference" between your income and spending rather than "spend the difference," which many people do. Review your budget each year. My wife, Debbie, and I review our investment portfolio, budget, income, insurance, and savings plan at least once per year. This is easy to do when you plan it out in advance. We even celebrate afterward with a date night dinner. The meeting usually takes place in early January like a "State of the Union." We set goals for the year, adjust our budget accordingly, and plan for vacations and other important events throughout the year on our calendar. Finally, we adjust our spending and savings accordingly and make sure we are still on track with our personal retirement race.

When you "follow the money" by checking your expenses and bills, you can see exactly where you are spending your money. Annual budgeting will help you better realize how much you are spending on going out for lunch and/or dinner, and how many $5 coffee drinks you are charging to your account each month. Realizing where the money is going sometimes changes your spending habits and will allow you to spend less and save more. Remember, it all adds up and will make a difference (especially over thirty to forty years) in your retirement race.

The following is a hypothetical budget, or typical list of common expenses most people have at some point in their life. Hopefully when you retire you have no debt (mortgage, car loan, credit card, or student loans), but either way you should budget accordingly. Those who have no debt in retirement usually have a less stressful retirement from an income needs standpoint.

Expense Budget

ITEM	MONTHLY	ANNUALLY
Mortgage/Rent		
HO/Renters Insurance		
Property Taxes		
HOA Fees		
Water		
Power/Electricity		
Lawn Care/Pool Care		
Lawn/Home Pest Control		
Home Maintenance		
TV (Cable, Sat)/Internet		
Cell Phone/Landline		
Car/Lease Payment		
Car Maintenance		
Car Insurance		
Gasoline (Fuel)		
Groceries		
Household Items		
Clothing		
Eating Out		
Going Out		
Entertainment		
Pets		
Hobbies/Sports		
Travel		
Memberships		
Charitable Giving		
Health Insurance Premiums		
Medical (Out Of Pocket)		
Life Insurance Premiums		
Gifts/Holidays		
TOTALS		

In our financial practice, we put together a list of expenses to help clients get started with calculating their current and future expenses. Hopefully this list will help you determine the income you will need to generate in retirement to cover these expenses and maintain your lifestyle.

Once you know what your expenses total, what is your other number? The number in the TV advertisement references the amount of savings you need when you retire. These savings should make your money last your lifetime while generating the consistent retirement income you need to maintain your desired lifestyle and spending habits. Wouldn't it be helpful if we could accurately calculate this number?

There are several retirement calculators available to help guide you on your retirement race plan. Some of these are available online. A financial advisor who specializes in retirement planning will likely have retirement planning software and tools that will help you build your plan while taking the following information into consideration:

- Annual income
- Annual savings (contributions to employer-sponsored retirement plans)
- Non-IRA savings such as to a bank savings account
- Assumed annual rate of return on both current investments and savings as well as future contributions
- Your monthly or annual expenses today with calculated annual inflation increases
- Your monthly or annual expenses in retirement (today's expenses, plus annual inflation, less expenses such as a paid off mortgage debt, contributions to a college savings plan, expenses of supporting minor children, etc.)
- Income sources in retirement (future pensions, Social Security, rental income, etc.)
- Future inheritance(s)
- Year-by-year withdrawal amount and withdrawal strategy incorporating the taxes to be paid

- Retirement income plan for a surviving spouse which should incorporate life insurance death benefits and adjustments to both future income and expenses moving forward

In our financial practice, we use a software program known as "Retirement Analyzer" to assist our clients in planning for, reaching, and maintaining their lifestyles in retirement. I can't emphasize to you enough how many pre-retirees today come into our office and struggle with determining how much money they are spending on a monthly and annual basis. This expense number helps us determine how much they can save toward retirement each year and, more importantly, how much they can spend on a monthly or annual basis in retirement. The expense number will also help us accurately determine how much they need to have saved to comfortably retire (remember that TV commercial?). These two figures (amount saved and expenses) are the basis for helping us put together a complete retirement savings and future income plan for our client's retirement.

Another important question to ask yourself is: where are you going to get income from once you are retired and potentially permanently unemployed? Some financial advisors refer to income in retirement as the three Ps of Retirement Income: **Portfolio**, **Protected**, and **Pensions**. **Portfolio** consists of your investment savings, much of which may or may not be invested in the stock market; **protected** refers to principal-protected investments or insurance such as cash, bank CDs, insurance backed annuities, etc.; and **pensions**, which offer lifetime income (corporate, state, or government pensions). Visually, the three Ps can also be explained using the three-legged retirement income stool analogy.

As I mentioned earlier in the book, my father-in-law was an executive for years with a large insurance company. He was a loyal and hard-working leader of the organization and stayed with the company for most of his career and then retired with a corporate pension that paid him a fixed income for the rest of his and his wife's lives. My in-laws have three streams of retirement income to draw from, including their corporate pension,

Social Security, and personal investments/savings. That is what we refer to as the three-legged retirement income stool.

Three-Legged Retirement Income Stool

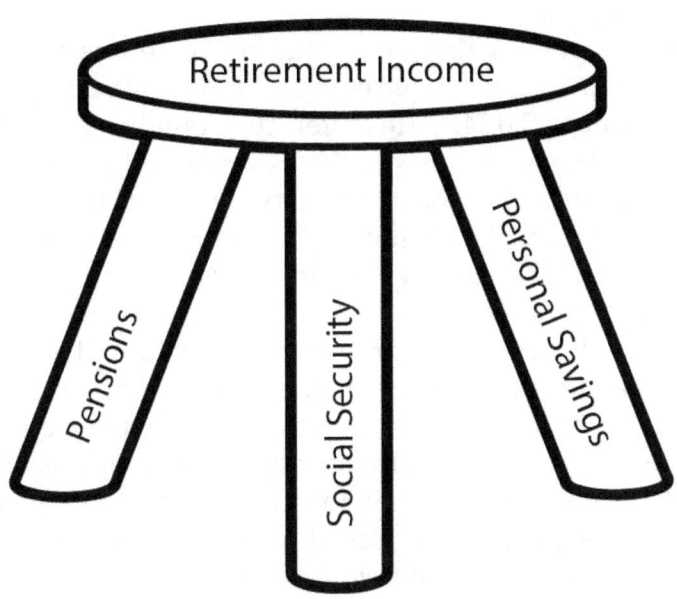

Today, most private companies and corporations do not offer their employees a pension they can rely on for income in their retirement years. To be fair, most employees also do not stay in one career or with one company throughout their working life. Federal and state government employees, military personnel, firefighters, police, teachers, and municipality workers still receive pensions, and these are great benefits for generating retirement income.

For most of us just starting out on our retirement race, the retirement income stool only has two legs. This does not sound very stable unless you are an acrobat. Corporations today have primarily replaced the traditional pension with various retirement savings plans, like the 401(k), allowing employees to make discretionary tax-deferred contributions for their retirement. As an incentive, many times the corporations will match the employee contributions up to a certain percentage, such as 3 percent. These plans now put the risk of investing for retirement and the responsibility to save for retirement on the individual employee.

Social Security is also a potential retirement income leg. At the time of writing, the average yearly Social Security income check is about $18,024.[11] However, the stability and reliability of this leg remains to be seen. We as working individuals continue to pay into the Social Security system, but projections show in a few years the outflows of paid Social Security benefits will outweigh the inflows of contributions that support the system.

The Social Security program was never intended to be the main source of retirement income, but today it often acts as the sole leg of income for those in retirement. With people living longer, the system has been financially strained; it was never intended to provide retirement income benefits for thirty-plus years for most people. The Social Security program will most likely be adjusted in the future for it to survive in its current form. One scenario may be that Social Security might be means tested in the future and based on some combination of your income and value of savings (assets) in retirement. If you are still working, you can log in to **www.ssa.gov** and see what your future benefits will be at full retirement. Based on the previously mentioned financial challenges and overall solvency of the Social Security program, you will likely find an estimated reduced future benefit (in percentage) noted on your personal statement.

What this really means for the younger investor planning for retirement is that we need to work harder on stabilizing the

---

[11] Brian Anderson. 401(k) Specialist. January 23, 2020. "20 Social Security Facts for 2020." https://401kspecialistmag.com/20-social-security-facts-for-2020/

retirement income stool, and in many cases creating a third leg to replace the missing pension and overcome reduced Social Security benefits.

For pre-retirees who do not have a corporate pension, one retirement income leg may consist of all your retirement savings in corporate plans like 401(k)s, plus additional savings in non-retirement accounts. The second leg will be your Social Security income, although it may be a reduced benefit.

When to take Social Security is a key decision for America's elderly, for whom the program has become a critical safety net. About half of older Americans get most of their retirement income from the program. According to a study in 2019, many retirees seem to claim Social Security benefits at the exact wrong time, which means that they could potentially miss out on collectively $3.4 trillion in benefits before they die.[12]

Current law states that if you qualify, you can start claiming benefits at age sixty-two. However, your benefit check will increase by 8 percent between age sixty-two and age seventy for every year you delay taking benefits. For example, a person eligible for a $725 monthly check at age sixty-two could get a $1,280 monthly check if they wait to start Social Security benefits until age seventy.

Americans are woefully under-educated when it comes to Social Security, according to studies from the Government Accountability Office, the AARP, and the Financial Literacy Center. Only 4 percent of U.S. retirees are waiting until age seventy to claim Social Security, which maximizes their monthly benefit. Meanwhile, more than 70 percent start taking reduced benefit checks before age sixty-four. If you are healthy and expect to live a long time, you might want to maximize benefits received later in life by delaying. Everyone's retirement timeline and personal situation is different and can affect the decision of when to start

---

[12] CBS News. June 28, 2019. "Almost All Americans Take Social Security at the Wrong Time, Study Says." https://www.cbsnews.com/news/study-says-retirees-lose-more-than-100k-by-claiming-social-security-at-the-wrong-time/

taking Social Security, so think about your own needs and make the choice that best fits your situation and goals.[13]

As you approach retirement, you might want to also consider converting some of your retirement savings into an annuity, which can provide you a guaranteed income stream that is reliable and that you cannot outlive. This strategy can act as the third leg of your retirement income stool and potentially replace that missing pension. This income strategy could provide you with a more stable and reliable income in retirement.

Bucket Planning in Retirement

When putting together a growth or growth and income plan, we believe in dividing your money and investments into three buckets. These buckets are differentiated based on liquidity, investment timelines, type of investment accounts, taxability, and types of individual investments based on investment goals.

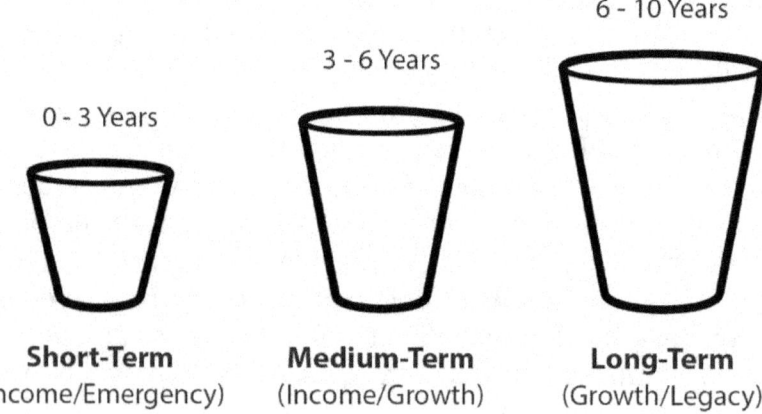

INVESTMENT BUCKETS

0 - 3 Years — **Short-Term** (Income/Emergency)
3 - 6 Years — **Medium-Term** (Income/Growth)
6 - 10 Years — **Long-Term** (Growth/Legacy)

---

[13] Janna Herron. USA Today. June 28, 2019. "Doing This One Thing with Your Social Security Could Mean Losing $100,000 in Retirement." https://www.usatoday.com/story/money/2019/06/28/social-security-claim-too-early-and-lose-100-000-retirement/1572620001/

Short-Term Bucket

You should have money in your short-term bucket that you might need to access for an emergency, regular day-to-day management of your household, and immediate income needs. For many people, the short-term bucket is money you have access to over the next three years. Your investments and savings should be geared toward this timeline. Investments in your short-term bucket are in most cases non-retirement types of accounts and often include checking, savings, and money market accounts. It is very important to have a savings account that will replace lost income if you temporarily lose employment for a period of time. Building up a three- to six-month cash or cash-like emergency fund that you can access will protect you during a severe financial hardship, temporary job loss, or pandemic.

Medium-Term Bucket

In your medium-term bucket, you should have money that is accessible in the next three to six years. The investments in the medium-term bucket, depending on your personal situation (age, retirement timeline, etc.), may be geared for growth and/or income. Investments in your medium-term bucket may include investments that generate interest and dividends that can help replenish the short-term bucket over time as it is depleted. The medium-term bucket many times will be composed of non-retirement accounts, including securities in a non-IRA brokerage account or retirement account.

Long-Term Bucket

In your long-term bucket, you should have money that you might need to access six or more years in the future. The investments in your long-term bucket, depending on your situation, will usually be geared for long-term growth or future income. Investments in your long-term bucket include your retirement accounts like company sponsored 401(k) plans, personal IRAs, and Roth IRAs. The investments in these accounts may have more risk, but your timeline to access the principal is generally longer. For many people, we refer to this bucket as the legacy bucket because this may be money you never spend in your lifetime and eventually pass on to your beneficiaries. The long-term bucket could also include investments that are geared for growth today with the idea of providing future income in retirement.

CHAPTER 6

TAX PLANNING

Benjamin Franklin once eloquently stated, "Nothing is certain but death and taxes." Well, if taxes are certain, then we should do some tax planning prior to retirement so that the taxes don't lead to our death.

Since most people save and invest primarily to create a comfortable retirement, you will want to choose investments that one day will help maximize your retirement income. Part of the planning of maximizing income means dealing with future taxes. Knowing when your income will be taxed is only half of the battle. You will also need to know what the tax rate for your future income will be. Unfortunately, it is impossible to accurately predict the future tax rates to which your money will be subject. To get a better idea of where the tax rates might be headed, let's look at the current economic landscape and the rising national debt. You should also consider looking at historical U.S. tax rates, including the recent changes made in the past several years.

Federal Deficit and Debt

The national debt is how much the United States owes to its creditors, while the deficit represents the yearly growth of the national debt. The deficit is how much more the U.S. spends than it earns. According to **www.usdebtclock.org**, in mid-2020 the United States eclipsed the $26 trillion debt mark.[14]

If the government reaches its debt ceiling, it will no longer be able to borrow money to meet its obligations. It can either reduce the deficit by a combination of increased tax revenue and decreased spending, or it can default on any number of its obligations. Most economic experts believe that a default would be disastrous, resulting in a hit on the government's credit rating, higher interest rates, higher prices on consumables, and inflation. Therefore, Congress has continued to increase the debt ceiling as the national debt reaches this level so it can spend more, which adds to the overall national debt.

However, just because Congress continues to allow the government to borrow as much as it can doesn't mean there is a limit. If the government's debt becomes too high in relation to GDP (gross domestic product), its credit rating might get lowered, resulting in problems like those associated with a default. Does this mean that tax hikes and budget cuts are imminent? As of 2019 the debt-to-GDP ratio sits at 105.5 percent.[15] Experts contend that the debt-to-GDP ratio should be no higher than 80 to 90 percent and probably closer to 60 percent.[16] If GDP doesn't grow at a fast enough rate to bring the debt-to-GDP ratio down to an appropriate level, the U.S. government would have to decrease or even eliminate the yearly deficit. There are two primary means of increasing tax revenues:

1. Increase the tax rates, and
2. Broaden the tax base

Many experts believe the national debt has reached such enormous levels that tax rate increases are imminent, since the debt needs to be paid off with tax revenue.

---

[14] usdebtclock.org. 2020.
[15] Federal Reserve Bank of St. Louis. July 26, 2019. "Gross Federal Debt as Percent of Gross Domestic Product." https://fred.stlouisfed.org/series/GFDGDPA188S
[16] Reuters. October 22, 2013. "Fitch: 80%-90% Debt to GDP Usually Maximum for 'AAA' Sovereign Ratings." https://www.reuters.com/article/fitch-80-90-debt-to-gdp-usually-maximum/fitch-80-90-debt-to-gdp-usually-maximum-for-aaa-soverign-ratings-idUSFit67222220131022

Federal income tax rates increased slightly back in 2013 with the end of the Bush tax cuts, remained level for several years, and then were decreased again under President Trump's tax reform act. Tax rates in 2019 are extremely low compared to historical tax rates. Between 1982 and 1986, income tax rates reached as high as 50 percent. Before that, the top rates reached 70 percent and at one point in time as high as 94 percent, largely due to WWII. There has been a historical correlation between the national debt-to-GDP ratio and tax rates. For example, the debt-to-GDP ratio increased due to WWI and the federal income tax rates. Then came the roaring twenties and the debt-to-GDP ratio decreased along with income tax rates. The Great Depression followed, then WWII, bringing higher debt-to-GDP ratios along with higher tax rates (reaching levels over 90 percent). The tax rates stayed relatively high (70 percent for top earners) as the debt-to-GDP levels decreased until the early 1980s.

Since the early 1980s, the debt-to-GDP ratio has generally continued rising, but the tax rates have decreased or stayed level with one exception in the 1990s, when the highest tax rates increased from 31 percent to 39.6 percent and the debt-to-GDP ratio declined temporarily. In the 2000s, the United States faced wars and a major recession. We are currently experiencing the highest debt-to-GDP ratio since the aftermath of WWII. Tax rates are currently less than half what they were back then. While there are many more political and economic factors that affect our tax rates, the trends and history suggest that the low tax rates of the 2000s will one day be a thing of the past. With a growing national debt and a growing national deficit, it is critical for future retirees to plan properly for the potential for higher tax rates in the future. Higher taxes in the future will translate to less after-tax income available for you to meet your monthly expenses in retirement, so let's implement some tax strategies today that are designed to lower your taxable income in the future, so you have more after-tax money to spend in retirement.

Taxability of Investment Accounts

There are three different types of investment accounts when it comes to taxability: **Tax-Deferred** (pay taxes later), **Taxable** (pay taxes now), and **Tax-Free** (pay taxes never). I bet you can guess which one sounds the most appealing.

All your pre-tax retirement accounts including qualified plans such as 401(k)s, 457(b)s, 401(a)s, 403(b)s, and traditional IRAs make up your tax-deferred (pay taxes later) accounts. Retirement money makes up a great deal of most people's savings. According to a 2015 report, Americans had nearly $25 trillion in retirement savings.[17] In fact, the great majority of retirement savings is made up of pre-tax money sitting inside of IRAs or in employer-sponsored retirement plans, Section 401(k), or Section 403(b) accounts. The federal government has created income tax incentives for taxpayers to save money in such accounts. In some cases, employers offer company contribution matches.

Pre-tax retirement savings is money that you saved but never paid taxes on. You received a tax deduction upfront in the year that you made the contribution, and the good news is that these accounts grow tax-deferred (you do not pay taxes on the gains or principal as it grows) until you withdraw the money. The growth takes advantage of the power of deferral. You earn money on the money you would have paid taxes on. The bad news is that each dollar you take out of these tax-deferred accounts is taxable as ordinary income in your tax bracket in the year you withdraw the money. And if you withdraw it before age fifty-nine-and-one-half, you are usually subject to an additional 10 percent federal tax penalty (there are exceptions).

You may have been told to sock away as much as you can into your 401(k)s or other company-sponsored retirement plans while you were working because when you retire you would be in a lower tax bracket. Unfortunately, this is not always true. The reality is, many of our retired clients are getting good

---

[17] Nick Thornton. Benefits Pro. June 30, 2015. "Total Retirement Assets Near $25 Trillion Mark." https://www.benefitspro.com/2015/06/30/total-retirement-assets-near-25-trillion-mark/

income via pensions and Social Security and every dollar they take out of their tax-deferred retirement account affects their taxes, sometimes driving their tax bracket higher. One could make the argument that, as a nation, we are facing a future financial crisis due to our trillions of dollars of debt ($26 trillion in mid-2020 and counting), rising health care costs, the increasing burden on both the Medicare and Medicaid programs, and a Social Security system that, unless changed, could become insolvent at some point in the future.

If we do quick and simple math on all of this, it sounds a lot like there is a good chance that taxes could be higher in the future and not *lower* in our country. I would look at your pre-tax accounts such as 401(k)s as a debt owed to the IRS. As an example, if you have $500,000 saved in your 401(k), then $350,000 of it is yours and $150,000 is what you owe to the IRS in taxes. If you have $1 million saved, then $700,000 is yours and you owe $300,000 to the IRS. If tax rates go up or tax brackets change, you will owe more to the IRS and get to keep less.

With that said, the prudent retiree should plan to have income flexibility in retirement. As stated previously, we believe retirees should plan on having three different buckets of investment savings from which to draw income. We can also look at having investments in three buckets from a taxability standpoint. The **Tax-Deferred** bucket includes pre-tax IRAs and other retirement or "qualified" accounts. The **Taxable** bucket holds non-qualified accounts and anything you'll have to pay taxes on this year, and the **Tax-Free** bucket includes Roth IRAs and anything else where, having paid taxes upfront, you don't have to continue paying taxes, even on the growth. Of course, given a choice, we would love to have all our money in tax-free accounts only, but this isn't generally feasible, since all accounts have different terms and conditions that wouldn't be suitable for 100 percent of our portfolio.

So what do these buckets look like? Many 401(k) plans today offer both a traditional (pre-tax) and Roth (post-tax) option within the plan. Most companies will also match contributions up to a percentage as a benefit and incentive for employees to properly save for their retirement. For example, if you contribute 3 percent of your salary to the retirement plan, the company may match 100 percent of your contributions, giving you an additional 3 percent (this is *free money*, by the way). It is a great idea to contribute at the very minimum the amount you will get matched by the company, as the match is free money. You will not pay taxes on contributions to the traditional side of the plan and the contributions will grow tax-deferred. When you make withdrawals in retirement, all the money will be taxed as ordinary income in the tax year it is withdrawn.

If the plan offers a Roth 401(k) option, you will pay the taxes on the contributions as you make them (so you do not get the upfront tax deduction); however, the contributions will grow tax-free and when you take the money out in retirement it will always be tax-free. This assumes you follow the terms of the account, which means taking withdrawals after age fifty-nine-and-one-half and once the account has been open for at least five years. If your company matches contributions, the company match will always go to the traditional side and not the Roth, so you will have both a tax-free and a tax-deferred bucket, as opposed to just tax-deferred.

If your plan does not offer a Roth 401(k) option, you may be eligible to contribute to a personal Roth IRA outside of the plan, depending on your individual income or combined income if you are married. In this case, you probably want to maximize contributions to the company plan up to the match (and get the free match money), then maximize your contributions to a personal Roth IRA.

"Tax-Deferred" Accounts (pay taxes later)

- Qualified plans
- 401(k)s
- 457(b)s
- 401(a)s
- 403(b)s
- Traditional IRA
- SEP IRA

- Simple IRA
- Tax-deferred annuities

It is worth noting that there are many different types of annuities, as I mentioned earlier in the book. Tax-deferred annuities grow on a tax-deferred basis. Owners of these types of insurance contracts pay taxes only on the profits when they make withdrawals, take a lump sum, or begin receiving income from the account. At that point, they pay taxes at their ordinary income tax rate on any profit they've received from the contract—not the principal. Annuities can be very useful for providing growth and income in retirement, and, as a reminder from our previous discussion, because they can be straightforward or complex, it's important to work with an advisor who is licensed and has experience working with annuities.

Taxable accounts include non-IRA brokerage (investment) accounts and bank savings accounts. Remember the savings rule of thumb: spend less than you make, then save the difference. Building up an emergency account, savings account, and non-IRA investment account over time should be part of the plan. You will pay taxes on the interest and dividends in the year that it is earned in these accounts, but these non-IRA accounts serve a purpose. Having a liquid emergency account first is critical both in your pre-retirement years and retirement years. The amount you place in this account will depend on your comfort level, but a general rule will be access to six months of income. Bank and credit union checking, savings, money market accounts, and CDs generally offer the safety of principal protection and FDIC insurance.

Examples of Taxable Accounts

- Individual or joint brokerage
- Bank or credit union checking
- Bank or credit union savings
- Bank or credit union money market
- Bank or credit union certificate of deposit (non-IRA)

Tax-free accounts are, as the name indicates, tax-free. We discussed earlier the Roth 401(k) option possibly available in your qualified plan at work. Contributing to an individual Roth IRA will not offer you an upfront tax deduction. However, your account will grow tax-free and any withdrawals/distributions you make will be tax-free, if you follow the terms of the account. The Roth IRA is a type of account that will allow you to better manage your taxable income in retirement. With a Roth IRA, you will not have to worry about a rise in tax rates, since these are tax-free accounts.

Tax-Free Accounts / Investments

- Roth 401(k)
- Roth IRA
- Municipal bonds
- Life insurance
- 529 college savings plans

Municipal bonds are debt obligations issued by a federal, state, or local government. When you invest in a municipal bond, you are essentially loaning money to the government entity in exchange for a set amount of interest to be paid over a predetermined period. At the end of the term, the full amount that you invested is returned to you. Interest earned from an investment is usually subject to ordinary income tax rates, but under the current rules, interest paid on municipal bonds is generally tax-exempt if the bonds are used to fund government projects constructed for the public good.

The federal taxation of municipal bonds can be complex. To add to the complexity, each state has its own laws governing municipal bonds. However, most states do not tax individuals on the interest arising from municipal bonds issued by that state. Many retirees have favored municipal bonds for the tax-free income benefit and credit worthiness of the state or government agency backing the bond.

The economic landscape is ever-changing. There are contribution limitations on many traditional investments like IRAs and 401(k)s. There's so much potential impact on your current and future income. With all this, you might be left wondering what options you have to create a more tax-efficient strategy.

Although I will cover life insurance later in this book in more entirety, as well as the features of life insurance that provide a death benefit, I do feel it is worth noting that life insurance can also be used as potential tax-free accumulation tool.

The Life Insurance Retirement Plan (LIRP) is an accumulation tool that shares many of the tax-free attributes of traditional retirement accounts such as the Roth IRA. Not only are income distributions truly tax-free, but they also don't contribute to the provisional income thresholds that trigger the taxation of Social Security benefits. The LIRP has additional characteristics that make it a surprisingly effective tool in helping you reach a lower tax bracket in retirement.

A LIRP is essentially a life insurance policy that is specifically designed to maximize the accumulation of cash within the policy's growth account. With a LIRP, you buy as little life insurance as required by the IRS rules, while stuffing as much money into it as the IRS allows. The LIRP offers different investment options within the policy including a fixed interest account, stock market mutual funds, and stock-market-based indexing options to enhance the tax-free growth.

Life insurance, and specifically the LIRP, is unique and can be considered its own asset class. The IRS code has allowed life insurance cash values and death benefit proceeds to receive several tax advantages. These advantages include tax-free death benefits, tax-deferred accumulation, tax-free distributions, and tax-free accelerated death benefits.

Tax-Free Death Benefit: Beneficiaries of an individual life insurance policy don't have to pay income taxes on the benefits, whether they take the death benefit as a lump sum or as a payment over time.[18]

Tax-Deferred Accumulation Potential: A life insurance policy's cash value growth is tax-deferred, meaning the policy

---

[18] Internal Revenue Service. 2007-13. Internal Revenue Code Section 101: Certain Death Benefits." https://www.irs.gov/pub/irs-drop/rr-07-13.pdf

owner won't pay income tax on any cash accumulation inside the policy.

Tax-Free Distributions: As long as a policy hasn't been overfunded to the point that it becomes a Modified Endowment Contract (MEC), any loans taken against its cash value are not subject to income taxes, although loans and withdrawals will reduce available cash values and death benefits.

Tax-Free Accelerated Death Benefits: If the insured becomes terminally ill, a portion of the death benefit may be paid out while the insured is still living. These tax-free "living benefits" are paid on a per diem or other period basis and are excluded from income tax up to a limit determined by the IRS, per IRS Section 7702B(b).[19]

Shortly after my children were born, I began researching the costs of post-high school education. My research pointed me into the direction of 529 college savings plans. I liked the advantages of saving for college with post-tax dollars and turning them into tax-free growth and tax-free distributions when used for secondary education costs including college tuition, school supplies, computer/internet expenses, room and board, etc.

529 college savings plans offer tax-free growth and tax-free withdrawals in certain circumstances. Congress created them in 1996 and they are named after section 529 of the Internal Revenue Code. "Qualified tuition program" is the legal name.

There are two basic types of such college plans. The first is a prepaid tuition plan, and the second type is a savings plan. And each state has its own unique plan. States are permitted to offer both types.

All fifty states and the District of Columbia sponsor at least one type of 529 plan. This type of savings plan is operated by a state or educational institution, and offers tax advantages and potentially other incentives to make it easier and more economical to save for college. It's not just college, though. 529s also apply to other post-secondary training, or for tuition in connection with enrollment or attendance at an elementary or secondary

---

[19] Internal Revenue Service. 1998. Internal Revenue Service Code 26 CFR Part 1." https://www.irs.gov/pub/irs-regs/td8792.pdf

public, private, or religious school for a designated beneficiary, such as a child or grandchild. Contributions to a 529 plan are not tax deductible, but these plans offer other tax advantages.

The main advantage of this plan is that earnings are not subject to federal tax and generally are not subject to state tax when used for the qualified education expenses of the designated beneficiary, such as tuition, fees, books, and room and board at an eligible education institution and tuition at elementary or secondary schools. As stated, the upfront contributions to a 529 plan, however, are not tax deductible for federal tax purposes.

As of 2018, the term "qualified higher education expense" includes up to $10,000 in annual expenses for tuition in connection with enrollment or attendance at an elementary or secondary public, private, or religious school. This will allow you to save and pay for education prior to college/trade school, etc. The cost of tuition at many private elementary, middle, and high schools today can sometimes be as much as the cost of tuition at many colleges.

My now-eleven-year-old daughter Cassie works in our office during winter breaks and summer breaks from school. She loves getting dressed up, welcoming clients to the office, and being part of the team. Cassie is incredibly organized and already quite the planner. She has written several "marketing" pieces for the firm and writes the loveliest get-well cards for our clients dealing with sickness or injury. She is beginning to understand the value of money and the cost of higher education. I pay her $20 for a full day of work at the office. She came into the office one day during the summer months and, as we loaded up the car at the end of the day for our ride home, I pulled $20 out of my wallet and gave it to her as I usually do, and thanked her for her hard work and contribution to the firm. We discussed income and expenses and the rising costs of college and education on our commute home. By the time we arrived at the house and pulled into the garage, she handed me back the $20 and asked me to put it into her college fund. We both learned a lot that day about saving money. I was so proud of her.

One of the advantages of 529 college savings plan is that contributions are flexible. You can start off with a small lump sum of money, add to it at any time, set up monthly auto contributions, or just add to the plan around the holidays and birthdays. Grandparents, uncles, and aunts can also contribute money toward the education of their little loved ones. Education is a very special gift, especially when it is tax-free.

While market diversification is a fundamental investing strategy, tax diversification is not always addressed in financial discussions. It is important to examine your investments and insurance holdings both now and in the future, as your retirement race could be impacted by an uncertain and potentially costly tax environment. Nobody can predict what taxes will be in the future, however, looking at the state of our nation's economic affairs today including our ever-increasing national debt, it's definitely not a stretch to expect tax hikes coming our way in the near future.

Having retirement savings in each of these three different types of accounts (tax-deferred, taxable, and tax-free) will allow you and your financial advisor the flexibility to put an income plan together that takes taxes into account in retirement. This type of income plan will have the advantage of being able to manage your taxes and provide you with more after-tax income in retirement, regardless of future income tax rates and tax brackets.

CHAPTER 7
ESTATE PLANNING

I believe there are two main reasons people do estate planning. They love somebody as much as they love themselves, or they hate paying taxes. Estate planning is the collection of prepared tasks that serve to manage an individual's assets in the event of their incapacitation or death. These tasks include things like the bequest of assets to heirs and the settlement of estate taxes. In very simple terms, it is the orderly disposition of your assets upon your death to your heirs. Some of the major estate planning tasks include the following:

- Creating a last will and testament
- Limiting estate taxes by setting up trust accounts in the name of beneficiaries
- Establishing a guardian for living dependents
- Naming an executor of the estate to oversee the terms of your will
- Creating/updating beneficiaries on plans such as life insurance, IRAs, and 401(k)s
- Setting up funeral arrangements
- Establishing annual gifting to reduce the taxable estate
- Setting up a durable power of attorney (DPOA) to direct other assets and investments
- Setting up a health care surrogate appointing someone to make health care decisions for you if you are unable

- Establishing a living will which make your wishes known as to what quality of life you wish to maintain if you have a terminal condition, end stage condition, or are in a persistent vegetative state

Estate planning is an ongoing process, but one you should start as soon as you have any kind of measurable assets. As life progresses and goals shift, the estate plan should also be adjusted to be in line with your new goals. Lack of adequate estate planning can cause undue financial burdens to your loved ones (estate taxes can run higher than 40 percent). At the very least, a last will and testament should be set up even if the taxable estate is not large. Ancillary documents such as a durable power of attorney for assets, a health care surrogate, and a living will are documents that all adults should have regardless of financial status or position.

There are many important decisions you need to make when it comes to your estate: choosing who you want to leave your estate to, when they should get your assets (immediately at your death in a lump sum, or in pieces over several years), who you wish to appoint to follow your instructions at death, and who you want to make financial and health care decisions for you while you are alive. All of these decisions can be very difficult and many times will paralyze you from getting anything in place at all.

When clients struggle with these decisions, we often say something like this: Imagine you are living your last day. You have no estate planning documents in place, but you are granted the opportunity to make those final decisions and instructions before you die. What and who would you choose today? Remember that whatever you put in place today can be changed in the future. The reality is that life changes, people change, and circumstances change. Estate planning goals change, too. Not making advanced preparations today could significantly affect the people you love the most and leave behind at death. Not having these documents while you are alive could also negatively impact your financial well-being.

Probate

What is probate? Probate is the legal process of validating your last will and testament. The probate process can be costly and time-consuming. In fact, a lot of people believe that if they have a will, the settlement of their estate will be straightforward, inexpensive, swift, and uncompromising. The reality might be far from those beliefs. The actual costs of probate vary drastically from state to state. Costs run from 4 percent to 10 percent of the gross estate before any liabilities such as a mortgage or other debts are subtracted. Most estate planning organizations or legal firms use a flat fee of 5 percent of the estate when calculating potential probate costs. Most estimates put the American public's probate expenses somewhere around $2 billion annually, with about half of that dedicated solely to attorneys' fees.[20] By now you are probably asking yourself, how can I avoid probate? There are many ways to avoid probate. Each has their own tradeoffs, potential pitfalls, and set of costs. Now, it's important to note that I am not an attorney and do not provide estate planning services. However, let's review some probate avoidance options that you should consider and discuss with an attorney.

Using Beneficiary Designations

On your qualified retirement plans, you can designate a beneficiary or beneficiaries. If your beneficiaries are living when you pass on, the account will avoid probate and your assets will be distributed directly to the named beneficiaries. This beneficiary designation can also be done on your IRA, Roth IRA, and life insurance accounts. You can also designate direct beneficiaries on your non-IRA accounts such as bank checking, savings, money market, and CD accounts using what's called a "TOD" or "POD"

---

[20] Gudorf Law Group. Dayton Estate Planning Law. April 7, 2016. "Powerful Statistics about Probate." https://www.daytonestateplanning-law.com/powerful-statistics-probate/

designation form available at most banks and financial institutions. Depending on the financial institution, the form may be called "TOD" (transfer on death) or "POD" (payable on death). Do not forget about your individual or jointly held non-IRA brokerage accounts. These accounts can also avoid probate if you designate beneficiaries using the "TOD" (transfer on death) or "POD" (payable on death) forms.

Using Special Deeds for Real Estate

You can convey a transfer of ownership on a property after you pass on using a specific type of property deed. This deed incorporates special language known as an "Enhanced Life Estate Deed" or "Lady Bird Deed."[21] This enhanced life estate deed will keep your property and ownership in your name while you are alive, but designate a beneficiary or beneficiaries after you pass on, while avoiding probate. Primary residence real estate is one of the most common assets probated. An attorney specializing in real estate or estate planning can assist you with creating the enhanced life estate deed if it is available in your state of residency.

Adding Your Children to Your Accounts

Some people think that adding their children to their accounts or to the deed(s) to their property is an easy and low-cost way to avoid probate. And this can be true for many; if you do add their name to your accounts or property you will most likely avoid probate. However, if you add your children to your bank accounts, brokerage accounts, or to the deed on your real estate, you will be opening yourself up to the potential creditors and lawsuits of your children. You will also be creating potential future tax liabilities for them (your heirs will miss out on the step-up in cost basis tax advantage at your death, as well as potential

---

[21] American Council on Aging. 2020. "How Lady Bird Deeds Protect a Medicaid Recipient's Home for Their Loved Ones." https://www.medicaidplanningassistance.org/lady-bird-deeds/

estate tax exemptions). In almost all cases, from my observations, this can become a costly method of avoiding probate.

Establishing a Revocable Trust

The single most important reason for having a living trust is to avoid probate. The knowledgeable family or individual will choose the living trust as a solution to holding assets and avoiding probate. A properly funded living trust is basically unchallengeable. The trust is "living" and can be changed during your lifetime. A good living trust offers several advantages, including the following:
- Estate settlement with a trust is private, not public
- Trust may offer additional estate tax exemptions
- Some trusts are valid in all fifty states
- Estate settlement with a trust is swift and efficient
- Can provide for minor or handicapped children
- Can protect the inheritance from beneficiaries' creditors, lawsuits, or divorces

Once you have established a revocable living trust, be sure that you properly fund the trust. In our practice, this is one of the most frustrating things we see when a potential client visits us and shows us their unfunded living trust. If you have created a trust and not transferred your assets into the trust, then you paid for an instrument to avoid probate *that will not avoid probate*. Remember, the trust should own all your non-IRA bank, savings, and investment accounts in order to avoid probate. The trust should also own your real estate, and any shares of ownership in a business, entity, company, or corporation. Don't forget checking accounts, savings accounts, CDs, safety deposit accounts, online bank accounts, savings bonds, your primary residence, rental properties, timeshares, and even the 529 college savings plans you may have set up for your children or grandchildren.

Depending on your family situation and personal wealth transfer goals, your living trust may also be the primary or contingent beneficiary of your qualified plans, IRAs, Roth IRAs, life insurance, and annuities. This can be accomplished by filling out a change of beneficiary form with each of the financial institutions or logging into your online account and making the elections electronically.

Think of the trust as one big moving truck that holds all your assets on it while you are alive. You are the trustee and the driver of the truck while you are alive. When you pass on, the truck gets a new driver (your appointed successor trustee) and the successor trustee then starts distributing the contents of the truck as per your wishes. Some people mistakenly believe that when you have a living trust, you lose control of your assets. In fact, with a living trust, you have more control over what happens to your assets both during your lifetime and after your death.

THE ESTATE PLANNING "MOVING TRUCK"

A few years ago, my adopted grandmother passed away at the age of ninety-two. She was an incredible woman who fled former East Germany in 1947 and landed in New York City in 1950. She was an incredible cook. She came to this country with nothing and gave it everything she had. She cooked all her life in restaurants and clubs while volunteering in the community and supporting several charities and local institutions. She knew the meaning of hard work. When she passed away, it was my family's first experience with losing a family member so close to home. The experience for all of us was emotionally difficult and challenging because of the sudden loss of life. My grandmother did us all a great favor by planning for the time when she would leave us. In reality, my mom helped her with all of the planning. She had a prearranged and prepaid funeral and a cemetery lot picked out. She told us what she wanted in terms of a funeral and celebration of her life. We put together her obituary with information about her life story detailed in one of her published cookbooks (we were lucky to have all that information, otherwise it would have been much more challenging for us). The process of planning your funeral may sound a little strange or uncomfortable, but you will be serving the people you love if you take care of these details in advance. When a loved one passes from this world, it is never the right time. Unfortunately, dying is a part of living, and eventually our time will come.

I have put together a short list of final instructions and general information you should make readily available for those you leave behind to help them with the process. You should keep this important information together along with your estate planning documents in a safe place that can be readily accessed by a loved one.

Final Instructions Checklist

- Pre-paid funeral arrangements (funeral home name and contact information)
- Explanation of what you wish your celebration of life to look like (hymns, prayers, flowers, etc.)

- Write your own obituary or life story
- List of all online accounts with login and password information
- List of all investment accounts (account numbers, log-in, and password if applicable)
- List of all bank accounts (account numbers, log-in, and password if applicable)
- List of all life insurance and long-term care insurance policies (account numbers, log-in, and password if applicable)
- List of all credit cards (account numbers, log-in, and password if applicable)
- List of any outstanding debts and/or creditors you may have (mortgage, student loans, etc.)
- Contact information for your accountant, attorney, doctors, church clergy, family, and friends
- Combination to your safe at home (if applicable)
- Passwords for computers, cellphones, electronics, etc.

Regardless of the estate planning road you choose to take, be sure to work with an advisor and/or estate planning attorney that will help guide you to the best solutions available for both you and your family. Once your estate plan has been established, be sure to review your wishes and estate planning documents on an annual basis so they are up to date from a legal standpoint and meet your current wishes. When is the best time to start working on your estate planning? Today, of course.

CHAPTER 8

LIFE INSURANCE

The main reason I own life insurance is because I love my family. Much like estate planning, there are really two underlying reasons people own life insurance. The first reason is because you love someone more than you love yourself. The second reason is because you hate to pay taxes. Life insurance comes in many shapes, colors, and sizes. Life insurance is a contract between an insurance policyholder and an insurer, or assurer, where the insurer promises to pay a designated beneficiary a sum of money in exchange for a premium upon the death of an insured person. Choosing the right type of life insurance can be very challenging and is almost like the difference between leasing and buying an automobile. You should work with a licensed advisor who can help you decide which type of policy will best address your needs and goals.

Whether you need life insurance or not is the first critical question you should ask yourself, and the answer will depend on your personal, ever-changing situation. Most people think only of death benefit protection when they think of life insurance. Certainly, the main purpose of life insurance is to help ease the financial burden for your family if you were to pass away prematurely. The death benefit can help replace your lost income, help the family cover the various taxes that may be due on your assets, and, of course, help with funeral and other final expenses associated with your passing.

Remember, life insurance death benefit proceeds pass on to your beneficiaries income-tax-free. This tax-free benefit can also make life insurance a very effective wealth transfer vehicle.

When my wife, Debbie, and I got married, we were both working and able to support ourselves individually and jointly. Life insurance was important, but not as important as it was after we started a family. Now, as a married father of two young children and the main source of income generation, it was and still is my responsibility and intention to protect my wife and kids in case something permanently happened to me. I wanted to ensure that life continues from a financial standpoint and my wife could take care of the children while providing the proper educational opportunities without worrying about the day-to-day finances. For me, the tax-free death benefit life insurance I chose was the best way to accomplish this goal.

There are several different types of life insurance available today. This can make finding the right insurance for you and your personal situation very confusing. There are two main categories of life insurance: cash value and term.

Cash value life insurance (also known as permanent life insurance) combines both insurance and a savings component. Some examples include whole life and universal life. Some advisors recommend cash value policies to clients to also invest for retirement, which can be costlier. The actual cost of insurance is usually higher with a cash value policy than with a regular term policy. With a cash value life insurance policy, there are marketing and sales commissions to keep in mind along with a potential "surrender charge" that may be levied if you decide to cancel your policy within the first ten years. There can also be substantial investment fees within the life insurance policy to consider. For example, in variable life and variable universal life, these fees can often be as much as 3 percent or more annually.

However, a properly structured cash value life insurance policy can provide several tax advantages previously discussed in the tax planning chapter of this book, including:
- Income tax-free death benefit for your beneficiaries
- Tax-deferred cash value growth potential
- Supplemental retirement income through tax free policy loans and/or cash value withdrawals

Term life insurance, on the other hand, offers a fixed tax-free death benefit that insures your (or another individual's) life for a fixed period such as ten, twenty, or thirty years. Once the term expires, you no longer have the insurance coverage. If you choose to not pay the premium during the term, the insurance just cancels (lapses). Term life insurance is a lower cost insurance alternative that allows you to protect your family from lost income for a specified period and allows you to save/invest the difference that you would have paid into a cash value policy. Depending on your age and circumstances, term life insurance may be the most bang for your buck regarding maximizing death benefit and minimizing cost.

When asked to list financial assets, many people include stocks, bonds, savings accounts, home equity, retirement accounts, etc. When it comes to their expenses the list usually includes mortgages, utilities, food, clothing, health insurance premiums, and life insurance premiums. While focusing on building assets for retirement, life insurance is oftentimes viewed as just a necessary expense to help protect a family's future. The reality is, life insurance can also be an asset in your overall financial strategy and retirement plan, offering you much more than just death benefit protection. Helping protect your family and knowing you are passing on a legacy to the people you love can give you both a feeling of assurance and comfort.

Evaluating your life insurance needs should not be a one-time event. Life is ever-changing, and so are your financial needs. Of the many instruments that make up a client's assets, life insurance is often the least monitored or reviewed. In our experience, life insurance policies should be reviewed every year to ensure they are performing as you expected and are aligned with your current financial goals and objectives. Make sure you regularly review the beneficiaries you have listed on your policy. There are certain life events that may trigger the need for an adjustment to your life insurance needs or coverage. The most common include:

- Change in marital status
- New home purchase
- Birth of a child or adoption
- Taking on debt
- Planning for college
- Planning for retirement
- Significant change in assets
- Change in a business ownership

Your individual situation will determine when and how often a review of your life insurance coverage is required. Remember to do a life insurance needs analysis as part of your overall retirement planning. Don't let sudden tragedy uproot your family or bankrupt your business. Even after you pass, there are still people who will rely on you. Life insurance can address all of this and more. You will sleep much better with life insurance.

CHAPTER 9

LONG-TERM CARE INSURANCE

My wife's grandmother, "Nanny," passed away in 2017 at the age of ninety-nine. Nanny grew up in Indiana and lived most of her life in Indiana and Central Florida. She was a very special and sweet lady who loved to go bowling, eat good food, and go to church. Nanny moved to an assisted living facility when she was ninety-two and lived there for the last seven years of her long life. Living into your eighties, nineties, or even to age one hundred is becoming more and more prevalent today, and can have a significant impact on your retirement plans and savings needs.

At least 70 percent of people over the age of sixty-five are expected to require some form of long-term care services and support during their lives, and the costs can be astounding.[22] Statistically, that means only 30 percent of the people over age sixty-five will not need some form of long-term care.

In 2019, the median annual cost for a semi-private room at a nursing home in Florida was over $102,565. The annual cost

---

[22] Richard W. Johnson. ASPE. April 4, 2019. "What is the Lifetime Risk of Needing and Receiving Long-Term Services and Supports?" https://aspe.hhs.gov/basic-report/what-lifetime-risk-needing-and-receiving-long-term-services-and-supports

for an average assisted living facility in Florida was a whopping $42,000 while the costs for full-time home health care runs approximately $50,336. These costs are even higher in larger metropolitan cities in our country. And it's also estimated that as time goes on, prices will only continue to rise.[23]

Because we are living longer, you should consider looking at different strategies to help protect you and your loved ones against a long-term care need, which could turn into a financial drain or burden.

Long-term care, or LTC, is a catchall term for services that provide medical and non-medical assistance to people who struggle to perform two or more Activities of Daily Living, or who have cognitive impairments like dementia.

The six ADLs include bathing, dressing, continence, eating, toileting, and transferring (moving oneself from a sitting to standing position such as getting in and out of bed). Long-term care comes in many different variations to accommodate the different levels of assistance one might need.

As you run your personal retirement race and get to the later mile markers in your fifties, sixties, and seventies, you should consider the different types of care you might need in the future and how you will fund it.

Most people believe a nursing home will take your assets. A nursing home is a type of place to live based on the level of care or nursing services you might need. A nursing home does not want your assets, it wants to get paid just like any other place you might stay or live. For example, in the early years of your life, you might pay rent to live in an apartment or house. At some point, you may purchase a condo or home and then pay a mortgage payment so you can live there. If you move to a retirement community you probably pay a monthly fee, entrance fee, and more. The same holds true for a long-term care or nursing home facility. The long-term care facility wants to get paid for providing a place to live and for the care you are receiving. The LTC facility does not want your assets.

---

[23] Genworth. 2019. "Cost of Care Survey 2019." https://www.genworth.com/aging-and-you/finances/cost-of-care.html

According to a Genworth Cost of Care Survey in 2019 the median annual cost for different types of services are as follows:[24]

- Homemaker services: $51,480
- Home health aide: $52,620
- Adult day health care: $7,500
- Assisted living facility: $48,612
- Nursing home semi-private room: $90,156
- Nursing home private room: $102,204

Now that we are a little more familiar with the different costs and services, we can look at things in a little more detail. We can do this by asking the question: Can you realistically preserve your retirement assets and income if you were to suffer long-term care costs? Let's look at the different ways you can pay for long-term care and weigh in on some of the pros and cons of each option. Clearly your individual situation must be considered with a financial professional before choosing an option. Statistically, not everyone will need care at home or at a long-term care facility, but those that will need care can be assured that it could be expensive and likely will not get any cheaper in the future. You should discuss the following options in detail with your trusted financial advisor so that you consider the costs and potential impact on your retirement while putting the proper plan in place.

Self-Insure

You can rely on your personal retirement savings and assets to cover the costs. At the current long-term care rates and projected increasing costs for care, you had better save diligently. Some people have reliable income in retirement which includes a pension and Social Security that together will go a long way towards paying for the cost of long-term care. Other self-insurers should designate a "bucket" of savings specifically aimed at

---

[24] Ibid.

paying for long-term care insurance protection. Self-insuring allows you to maintain control of your assets and the flexibility and freedom to choose the type of care you want. If long-term care costs escalate and your retirement assets shrink, you may risk depleting your retirement savings and your freedom to choose your care may become limited as retirement savings are reduced.

Rely on the Government

Medicare is a federal health insurance program for people who are sixty-five or older, certain younger people with disabilities, and people with end-stage renal disease. Medicare may pay up to one-hundred days of medically necessary care in a skilled nursing facility per benefit period, and the first twenty days are paid at 0 to 10 percent; however, a qualifying hospitalization must occur to activate this benefit. Days twenty-one through one-hundred will require a co-payment, and Medicare does not provide coverage for long-term care (also known as custodial care) with respect to any activities of daily living. Medicare does not provide any care or assistance that can help you remain in your home which is what most people wish to do. Once Medicare stops paying, any Medicare supplemental insurance policy will also stop paying. Remember that Medicare pays for acute care, but not for long-term residency.[25]

Medicaid is a health insurance program intended to help low-income and other vulnerable populations. It covers children, the aged, blind, and/or disabled and other people who are eligible to receive federally assisted income maintenance payments. The program is a joint federal- and state-government program, so eligibility for coverage and the particular requirements of the program vary based on what state you are in. Medicaid pays for some long-term care services, in home or in a facility, if you qualify for the program. For adults who need LTC, Medicaid requires that your assets and income are low enough

---

[25] Medicare.gov. "Skilled Nursing Facility (SNF) Care." https://www.medicare.gov/coverage/skilled-nursing-facility-snf-care

to make you eligible for the program. Once you spend down your assets to less than $2,000, Medicaid will take over the cost of long-term care. But, if Medicaid is your LTC fallback, be aware: Medicaid has a five-year look-back period for any assets someone may have gifted or transferred ownership in the previous sixty months. Trying to gift or transfer your assets away to qualify for Medicaid will result in either a penalty or a postponement of Medicaid qualification. Also, remember that being dependent on Medicaid limits your choices of quality care and the quality of facilities in which you will reside.

Traditional Long-Term Care Insurance

The concept of insurance is transferring risk to another party. Much like your homeowner's insurance, long-term care insurance is something you pay for and hope to never use.

Traditional long-term care insurance is a comprehensive insurance product that helps pay for the cost of long-term care. Long-term care insurance policies reimburse policy holders a daily amount up to a pre-selected limit for services to assist them with the activities of daily living (ADLs). Long-term care insurance is designed to cover long-term services, including personal and custodial care in a variety of settings such as your home, a community organization, or other facility.

Long-term care insurance helps you maintain your independence should an LTC event arise. The insurance allows you to better afford quality care. It reduces both financial and emotional stress that an LTC need may cause, and it may help you qualify for a long-term care partnership program. Long-term care partnership programs help protect assets that would normally need to be spent down prior to qualifying for Medicaid coverage once LTC benefits have been exhausted. Sometimes the premiums for LTC insurance can be tax deductible because LTC insurance premiums are considered a medical expense.

The problem with traditional long-term care insurance is the cost. The premiums rise with age, so the policies are less expensive when you are younger and more expensive in your later years. The premiums are also not static, so LTC policies can incur rate increases during the life of the policy as the costs for care increase. LTC insurance, like home or auto insurance, is a "use it or lose it" concept. If you do not have an LTC claim, then you will not receive any of your insurance premiums back. No one looks forward to the day that they get to use their LTC insurance. You should also consider that, prior to issuing a policy, health underwriting will be required, and some people do not qualify for the insurance as the insurance company is not looking to "buy a claim." As a rule, the older you get, the more likely you will not qualify for an LTC insurance policy.

Asset-Based Long-Term Care Insurance

This type of coverage is a life insurance contract with an optional long-term care benefit for certain long-term care needs. If care is not needed, then a death benefit will be paid out upon the insured's death. This type of insurance provides protection should a long-term care need arise. It also provides a tax-free death benefit to your beneficiaries when you die, but only if the policy has not been used or exhausted for long-term care expenses. The premiums for the long-term care benefit are usually guaranteed, so there will not be rate increases in the future. Existing savings can be used to fund (pay the premiums) the life insurance in a lump sum or over time. The policy will pay for qualifying long-term care expenses when or if they are incurred. If long-term care is not needed or if the policyholder dies, the policy's death benefit is transferred to the heirs (tax-free, in the case of life insurance).

This type of insurance protection does not qualify for a partnership program. Simplified health underwriting will usually be required prior to issuing a policy. One of the main advantages of asset-based long-term care insurance strategies compared with traditional LTC insurance is that your premiums won't completely "go to waste" because you will either use the protection during your life or your beneficiaries will receive a tax-free death benefit when you die. Either way, you won't get the premiums you paid for the LTC benefit back, but your policy's death benefit will remain intact. In our practice, this is what we often refer to as the "don't use, don't lose" long-term care insurance strategy.

When deciding on the correct path to take when trying to avoid a potential need for long-term care, your considerations will reach beyond the financial cost of care. You, your spouse, and your loved ones will be affected in many ways, including in your careers and personal lives. We've included the following statistics from a Genworth survey in 2016. It may be a little dated, but the point stands that a caregiving discussion goes well beyond funding options: [26]

Impact on Caregiver Careers

- 1/3 of caregivers provided thirty or more hours of care per week and half of them lost 1/3 of their income
- 77 percent of caregivers missed time from work

---

[26] Genworth. 2015. "Beyond Dollars 2015." https://www.hmgltc.com/downloads/BeyondDollars2015.pdf

Impact on Caregiver Quality of Life

- 43 percent of caregivers said that providing care impacted their own personal health and well-being
- 41 percent of caregivers experienced negative physical side effects such as depression
- 33 percent of caregivers reported an extremely high level of stress in their lives
- 45 percent of caregivers reported a reduction in their quality of living to pay for care

Financial Impact on Caregiver

- 62 percent of caregivers used their own savings and retirement funds to provide out-of-pocket financial assistance
- 11 percent of caregivers lost their jobs due to providing care

Thoughtfully consider which option, if any, is right for you as you progress toward old age. Making these hard decisions means you are protecting yourself and your loved ones should the need for long-term care arise in your future. Think about the potential impact a long-term care situation could have on your future caregiver, as well. Discuss your financial situation with a qualified advisor so that a long-term care situation does not abruptly derail your retirement race.

CHAPTER 10

QUESTIONS YOU SHOULD ASK

Finances can weigh heavily on your mind. Sometimes it is easier to deal with this stress on your own rather than talk to a financial advisor. In fact, that's exactly what most people are doing. Only about 17 percent of Americans meet with a financial advisor to help handle their finances and income.[27]

This means that around 75 percent of all Americans have not met with a financial advisor and are instead relying on their own knowledge and experience. This leaves much more room for guessing at certain expenses and less accountability in meeting financial goals.

We might have a retirement crisis on our hands due to the lack of preparation for retirement and the lack of guidance from professionals. Undoubtedly, there is a clear and growing demand for people to get in the retirement race and engage in long-term retirement planning.

Have you ever had to hire someone in an area that was not in your comfort zone or wheelhouse? It can be a scary feeling

---

[27] Jessica Dickler. CNBC. April 2, 2019. "75 Percent of Americans are Winging it When it Comes to Their Financial Future."
https://www.cnbc.com/2019/04/01/when-it-comes-to-their-financial-future-most-americans-are-winging-it.html

because you may not have all the pertinent information at your disposal to make an informed decision. Who do you hire? Who can you trust? Are you going to get ripped off? These are all fair questions and should be of concern to you.

In 2014, I purchased a house that needed some minor, but critical, repair work. There was a small leak in the roof that caused damage to a front window and seal. If not properly repaired, the damaged area could have caused additional wall damage and a potential mold problem in the house. Because I am hardly an expert when it comes to roofing, window repair, or construction in general, I looked for a skilled professional I could trust to do the repairs at a fair price. After all, our primary residence is arguably our most important asset, and improper maintenance could lead to other future problems. How did I find a trustworthy and competent professional? By doing a little homework, getting some professional referrals, and asking the right questions.

Wouldn't it be great if we always knew the right questions to ask when faced with an important decision or when seeking advice from someone who has knowledge, experience, and expertise? Choosing the right financial advisor to help plan your retirement and manage your money to meet your long-term financial goals is one of the most important decisions you will ever make. Not only will you be sharing your personal information with a virtual stranger, but you also will trust them to always act in your best interest with your money, your financial future, and the well-being of your family.

Some people don't want to work with an advisor or do not feel comfortable enough to work with a financial advisor and that is also okay. The do-it-yourselfers do their own investing and use the internet, books, articles, etc. to get their questions answered and help them along their retirement race. If you have the desire, acuity, and time, this is a viable approach. But for many, this can be a very difficult undertaking.

What if you are not working with a financial advisor or are not happy with your current advisor and wish to work with another financial professional to guide you to and through retirement? Clearly, a great way to find a trusted and competent advisor to help you with your retirement savings and income plan is through a referral from someone you respect who has had a great experience over time. Referrals are usually a great source any time you are looking to hire someone to do service work for you whether it be maintenance, professional, medical, etc.

What questions should you ask when interviewing that potential trusted advisor? I think it is safe to say that you can find the right answers if you know the right questions to ask. In our financial practice, over time we have compiled a list of fourteen important questions that you should ask when choosing a financial advisor to act as a trusted financial partner for you and your family.

1. How long have you been an advisor?

The knowledge and experience of an advisor who has weathered both good and bad markets will potentially be an asset to your long-term financial health. Ideally, it's preferable that the financial advisor has successfully managed through the technology stock bust of the early 2000s, the financial collapse and recession of 2008 and the most recent COVID-19 pandemic of 2020.

2. In what areas do you specialize?

Some advisors work with all ages of clients, including young people just starting out, and some specialize in working with people who are retired or close to retirement. If you are close to or in retirement, you may want to seek an advisor who specializes in these areas and specifically serves these types of clients. Remember, if you had a heart condition that needed attention, you would probably want to see a heart specialist, not just a general practitioner.

3. Are you a fiduciary?

Fiduciaries are held to a high legal duty and higher ethical standards because they have the responsibility of making financial decisions on behalf of the client or principal. They must hold the clients' best interests above their own when providing investment advice. As a fiduciary, an advisor must provide full disclosure regarding fees, compensation, and any conflicts of interest. If given a choice, I suggest you work with a fiduciary.

4. Do you have an office?

You want to seek an advisor who has an office that you can go to and visit. You do not want someone who works out of the back of their car and may not want an advisor who does not have a dedicated office or support staff to serve you.

5. How many people are on your team?

Let's face it. One person cannot do everything. Your financial advisor should not be the one to answer the phones, put in supply orders, and sign for packages while they are holding consultations and managing your money. Ideally, you want your advisor to have a staff who can manage the office while the advisor focuses on meeting with new and returning clients to help ensure their retirement is on track.

6. Do you have a sales manager?

Many brokers who work for large financial brokerage firms report to sales managers. Many times sales managers will dictate to the broker which funds or investments they should recommend to their clients. Whether the investment product is the best for the client might run at a distant second. Do you want a sales manager telling your financial advisor what investments to recommend for you? An independent financial advisor should work for you and not for a sales manager.

7. Does your firm have proprietary products?

This means the firm makes, recommends, and sells their own investment products. This would allow them to make money in more than one way. Proprietary products might allow the advisor and firm to make money on the investment product itself and charge a fee or commission on the actual sale of the product. If you are working with a large brokerage firm advisor, be sure to carefully review these types of investments if they are recommended to you against other potential solutions before you decide to buy.

8. What professional licenses do you currently hold?

The licenses the advisor holds determine what can be recommended and sold. If your financial professional holds only an insurance license, then insurance products such as annuities, life insurance, and long-term care insurance will be the only solutions suggested for you. This individual is considered an insurance agent only and is not a true "advisor." If your financial professional holds only a securities license, then stocks, bonds, and other securities will be the only solutions suggested for you. This individual is considered an investment broker only and is not a true "advisor." Working with an advisor who is registered to provide you with financial planning services may be in your best interest because this individual is considered a "true" financial advisor and can usually offer you a broader array of solutions to help meet your goals.

9. Have you ever been disciplined, sanctioned, or fined by any regulatory body?

You want to make sure the company or person you are selecting to be your financial advisor doesn't have a number of complaints against them. How can you check on something like that?

Go to the Better Business Bureau to search the company name and see if there are any complaints against the company. Another great resource is www.finra.org. You can go to the site and type in the broker's name in the "Broker Check" area. You will find out whether the advisor has ever been disciplined, sanctioned, or fined.

10. What is your investment philosophy?

Some investment strategies are based solely on the stock market, solely on insurance products, or perhaps a combination of the two. Alternatively, some investment philosophies are geared more towards growth than income or capital preservation. Make sure the planner's investment approach is a good fit and in alignment with your risk preference to reach your goals.

11. How do you evaluate the investments you recommend?

How does the individual or company select where your money should be invested? What kind of research is done to ensure that they are investing your money not only wisely, but to a legitimate company? Do they go and visit the companies they want to invest in to see how their business is run and meet with management? Do they do their due diligence? Has the advisor personally invested in the same investments they are recommending for you?

12. How do I know I can trust you (or anyone else)?

It is always helpful if you are referred by someone who has had a relationship with the advisor. Clearly, that does not protect you from the Bernie Madoffs of the world, but it can help weed out some of the bad apples. You can also protect yourself by ensuring that your money is held by a third-party custodian, bank, or trust company. The advisor should not have access to your money, nor do you ever want to make out a check directly to the advisor or advisory firm.

13. How do you get paid as an advisor?

There are really two different ways an advisor should or could get paid: commission-based, or fee-based. Many advisors, depending on the type of products they recommend, get paid via a combination of these two methods. It is important that you get full disclosure of all the fees in advance, so you are not surprised later. It is also important to ask the advisor if all your money is going to work for you or if some of it is going to pay them upfront. This is known as a sales load.

For example, if you are investing in mutual funds, you may want to consider no-load "C Shares" (which have no commission or early withdrawal penalty on your investment) as opposed to front-loaded "A Shares" (you are paying a commission up front when you invest your money) or back-loaded "B Shares" (you pay a penalty (deferred sales charge) if you withdraw your money prior to the end of a specific time period, such as six years). Assuming the mutual fund investments recommended are suitable for you, this will ensure that all your money is going to work for you. Owners of "C Shares" have flexibility to make changes in the investments without paying a penalty and the advisor's interest is aligned with yours. There may be occasions where other share classes may be in your best interest, but you deserve a reasonable explanation.

14. Do you have a business continuity plan? If so, what is it?

What happens to my investments if the advisor were to unexpectedly die or leave the business? Is there another advisor at the firm who is familiar with my situation and can help me with the transition? The right advisor or advisory team will have a business continuity plan in place for all of these scenarios, so your investments continue undisturbed, you will have access to move to another advisor or firm (if necessary), and you continue to receive service on the investment accounts.

Many of these questions are applicable to any type of advisor you are looking to work with, including doctors, lawyers, accountants, contractors, etc. As the co-founder of a financial advisory firm that specializes in assisting people who are close to retirement or currently in retirement, I can tell you that this is not always the easiest of decisions. I suggest that if you can find an advisor or advisory firm that offers a total wealth management approach and addresses the areas mentioned in this book your retirement will be much more assured and you will have a greater chance of successfully finishing your retirement race.

Remember Proverbs 15:22 from the Bible. *"Plans fail for lack of counsel, but with many advisers they succeed."* Find yourself an advisor or advisory team that is the best fit for you, and they can provide you with the "coaching" you need to successfully run your retirement race.

CHAPTER 11

THE FINISH LINE

You have crossed the finish line and are officially retired. Now what? Most people who are retired do not want to go back to work once they retire. In fact, we have seen many people count down their last days of work beginning two years out. We have also witnessed the opposite as clients decided to take a short break after retirement and then go back to part-time or even full-time work for several years.

When my son, Vaughn, received a trophy after he finished his race, we took pictures of him with his medal and celebrated his accomplishment. However, we had not yet gotten back to the car when Vaughn started planning for his next race the following weekend. Vaughn said that he could improve on his finish time and maybe even on his medal spot. My daughter Cassie was inspired by Vaughn's success, as well. She started training for her races and then won several trophies herself. We can all be inspired when reaching a goal and crossing the finish line.

For retirees, the next race may be the next phase or chapter in your life. It may be those life passions you never really had the time to focus on while you were working. It may be volunteering for a nonprofit, giving back to the community, mentoring children, learning to play a musical instrument, exercising, playing sports, coaching, travelling the world, reading, and so much more. It may also be that working is your passion and an integral part of your life. That is perfectly okay. In fact, it may be healthy to keep working. Perhaps you might work part-time, consult, or continue with your regular work schedule. Remember, some people may never be able to afford to fully retire, while others may never want to retire.

I remember a client sharing a personal story with us. Her last day of work was on a Friday. She woke up early the next Monday morning like she did for forty years, got ready for work, drove all the way there, and then realized in the parking lot that she retired and was no longer employed at the company. If you do something for forty-plus years, you tend to get in a habit, and habits can be hard to break. If it is a good habit or something you just plain enjoy, you may not want to entirely break it. Remember, when it comes to retirement, one day you are working and the next day you are not. For some people, if they're not ready, retirement can truly be a difficult life transition.

It's kind of like the transition from the school year to summer break. My daughter Cassie finished fourth grade back in 2019. Her last day of school was on a Friday in May. She usually wakes up on her own at 6 a.m., gets dressed, brushes her hair and teeth, and makes breakfast. I told you she was independent and organized. The bus picks up the kids at the end of our street at 7:08 a.m. sharp, so mornings at the Rauchegger house need to be organized, efficient, and structured. Otherwise, we "miss the bus."

The Tuesday following Memorial Day (which for us is the first official day of summer break) Cassie woke up at 6 a.m. and began her school morning routine. I ran into her in our kitchen as I was getting ready to leave for work at 7 a.m. Of course, I asked her why she was up so early. I told her that during summer break she could finally sleep in and relax a little. She said, "Daddy, I can't help it, but my body and my mind are still programmed to wake up for school."

How do you respond to that? Cassie was right. It does take time to transition from the school year schedule to summer break time. The same holds true when we transition from our working lives into retirement life from both a physical and psychological standpoint. The transition to retirement can be that much harder since we are many times breaking a thirty-year to forty-year habit.

In our financial practice, we have worked with hundreds of families planning for, transitioning to, and managing their retirements. It is a big responsibility that we do not take lightly. For many retirees, the time they spend in retirement will become a third of their total lifetime. I can honestly say that every person and situation is different. Everyone runs their own retirement race and has their own individual finish lines.

Having assisted with so many retirements over the years, we have determined one consistent underlying theme: The common denominator of an enjoyable retirement is your ability and decision to spend time on the things you enjoy the most and with the people you love. I hope you have a great and successful retirement race!

Investment Advisory Services offered through Cramer and Rauchegger, Inc., a SEC Registered Investment Advisor.

PICTURES

THE RAUCHEGGERS, 2017

(from left: Vaughn, Debbie, Tom, and Cassie)

A DAY AT THE OFFICE WITH CASSIE

PREPARING FOR THE 2030 WORLD CUP

RACE DAY WITH CASSIE & VAUGHN

ABOUT THE AUTHOR

Tom Rauchegger was born in New York City and is a first-generation American. His parents, John and Emma Rauchegger, immigrated to the United States from Austria and Germany, respectively, in their early twenties to live the American Dream. Tom played competitive soccer and golf growing up and lived in Austria, New York, and Florida as a young boy and teenager.

In 1990, Tom graduated from Stetson University in DeLand, Florida, with a Bachelors of Business Administration. He spent most of the 1990s living in Germany while working in the global markets. Tom continued his soccer career while in Germany and played for FSV Hoehenrain in the Bavarian Soccer League. Tom gained valuable international experience while working with a clientele that spanned over thirty countries. His travel to over twenty-five countries gave him both an appreciation for the United States as well as a more global view on culture, people, business, and finances.

Upon his return to the United States, Tom received a Master of Business Administration in 1998 from the University of Central Florida Executive MBA program in Orlando, Florida. He graduated Beta Gamma Sigma in the honor society of the school of business. Tom is fluent in German and keeps the traditions of his family, background, and heritage.

Tom met his wife, Debbie, after moving back to Florida from Europe. They have two children, Cassie and Vaughn, and reside just north of Orlando in the town of Heathrow. Tom still enjoys playing competitive indoor and outdoor soccer (when his body allows) and coaching his kids' sports teams. Tom is an experienced financial advisor with both securities and insurance licenses, a Registered Investment Advisor, and the co-founder of the financial advisory firm Cramer & Rauchegger, Inc. He established the advisory firm in the early 2000s with his very good friend, soccer teammate, and business partner, Scott Cramer. The firm focuses on assisting families with their retirement and estate planning, the transition into retirement, and the management of their finances and estate planning throughout retirement.

Neither Cramer & Rauchegger, Inc. nor its representatives or employees offer tax, legal or estate planning services. Always consult with qualified tax/legal advisors concerning your own circumstances.

ACKNOWLEDGMENTS

I want to thank my friend and business partner, Scott Cramer, for contributing the foreword to this book and for inviting me to join him in co-founding our financial advisory practice. We met on the soccer field years ago as teammates. We continued the teamwork off the field as we built an advisory practice to assist families with their retirement planning. I truly appreciate the knowledge and expertise you shared with me as well as the business opportunity you extended to me. You are still my favorite goalkeeper, an integral part of our family (Uncle Scott), and a great friend.

    I want to thank all the many financial advisors and financial organizations throughout the country that I call friends, partners, and colleagues. I appreciate you graciously sharing your knowledge and expertise with me over the years. We have studied together, learned side by side, and shared information with each other in small groups, on advisory councils, and at educational conferences. You have inspired me to share our knowledge and stories throughout this book with people who are serious about their financial futures and retirement plans.

    I want to thank the many great families I have had the pleasure of knowing and working with over the years in our advisory practice. Only some of your personal stories are contained in this book, but all your stories are etched in my memory and have become part of my life. Thank you for choosing our firm and allowing me to be a part of your family and your retirement.

~ Thomas Michael Rauchegger

www.ingramcontent.com/pod-product-compliance
Lightning Source LLC
Chambersburg PA
CBHW070658220526
45466CB00001B/497